W9-CDZ-543

READ WELL®

Bats

Teacher's Guide

Unit 14

-al
·
as in anim<u>al</u>

-ible
·
as in flex<u>ible</u>

Note: See New and Important Objectives on page 2 for a complete list of skills taught and reviewed.

Critical Foundations in Primary Reading

Marilyn Sprick, Ann Watanabe, Karen Akiyama-Paik, and Shelley V. Jones

Sopris West®
EDUCATIONAL SERVICES

A Cambium Learning® Company

BOSTON, MA • LONGMONT, CO

ISBN 13-digit: 978-1-60218-537-1
ISBN 10-digit: 1-60218-537-9

7 8 9 10 11   B&B   16 15 14 13 12

166975/6-12

Table of Contents
Unit 14
Bats

Table of Contents

Letter Sounds and Combinations

Cumulative Review of *Read Well 1* Sounds and Combinations (Ss, Ee, ee, Mm, Aa, Dd, th, Nn, Tt, Ww, Ii, Th, Hh, Cc, Rr, ea, sh, Sh, Kk, -ck, oo, ar, wh, Wh, ě, -y as in fly, Ll, Oo, Bb, all, Gg, Ff, Uu, er, oo as in book, Yy, a schwa, Pp, ay, Vv, Qq, Jj, Xx, or, Zz, a_e, -y as in baby, i_e, ou, ow as in cow, ch, Ch, ai, igh, o_e, ir) and:

Unit 2	Unit 3		Unit 5	Unit 6
aw /aw/ **Paw** Voiced	**ew** /ōō/ **Crew** Voiced	**ue** /ōō/ **Blue** Voiced	**u_e** /ōō/ **Flute** Bossy E Voiced	**ow** /ōōō/ **Snow** Voiced (Long)	**ge** /j/ **Page** Voiced

Unit 6	Unit 7		Unit 8		Unit 10
-dge /j/ **Badge** Voiced	**ci** /sss/ **Circle** Unvoiced	**ce** /sss/ **Center** Unvoiced	**kn** /nnn/ **Knee** Voiced	**ph** /fff/ **Phone** Unvoiced	**oa** /ōōō/ **Boat** Voiced (Long)

Unit 11		Unit 12		Unit 13
oi /oi/ **Point** Voiced	**ea** /ěěě/ **Bread** Voiced (Short)	**gi** /j/ **Giraffe** Voiced	**au** /au/ **Astronaut** Voiced	**oy** /oy/ **Boy** Voiced

Affixes (including morphographs—affixes taught with meaning) and Open Syllables

Cumulative Review of *Read Well 1* Affixes (-ed, -en, -es, -ing, -ly, -s, -y, -tion) and:

Unit 2	Unit 3		Unit 5		Unit 6
re- **Means again** as in reread	**un-** **Means not** as in unhappy	**ex-** as in excited	**o** Open syllable /ō/ as in open and moment	**-ful** **Means full of** as in colorful	**bi-** **Means two** as in bicycle

Unit 7	Unit 8	Unit 11	Unit 12	Unit 13	
de- as in detective	**-able** as in comfortable	**i** Open syllable /ī/ as in silence and pilot	**be-** as in before	**-ous** as in enormous	**dis-** as in discover

Unit 14		Unit 15		Unit 16	
-al as in animal	**-ible** as in flexible	**-or** **Means one who** as in actor	**-ment** as in apartment	**-ic** as in scientific	**pre-** **Means before** as in preview

Unit 17		Unit 18		Unit 19	
-ity as in activity	**-sion** as in permission	**-ness** as in fairness	**-less** **Means without** as in helpless	**in-** as in insert	**im-** **Means not** as in impossible

Introduction
Bats

Story Notes

Are they birds? Are they mammals? Bats are the stars of this unit.

The War Between Birds and Mammals: Grandfather and Gray Cloud return for another American Indian legend, "The War Between Birds and Mammals." This legend also features a trickster, Bat, who uses his unique characteristics to pretend to be both bird and mammal.

The Incredible Flying Machine: Students learn more about the habits and distinctive qualities of the remarkable bat. Today, scientists are studying these small creatures with the hope of creating a bat-like flying machine.

A Bat's Life: Students build fluency with a poem that celebrates a bat's life.

Recommended Read Alouds

The *Read Well 2* suggested Read Alouds enhance small group instruction—providing opportunities to further build background knowledge and vocabulary.

> **CAUTION (Reminder)**
> Do not read the Read Aloud recommendations during small group instruction. Reserve this time for students to read.

The Great Ball Game by Joseph Bruchac
Folktale • Narrative

This is an outstanding retelling of a Native American folktale by celebrated American Indian author Joseph Bruchac. In this story, we learn how the outcome of a great ball game between the birds and the rest of the animals would change everything.

Read Well Connections
Students can compare the two versions of the conflict between the birds and the mammals. The Read Aloud presents an alternative to fighting to resolve the conflict.

NOTE FROM THE AUTHORS

BAILEY PHELPS, MASTER STORYTELLER

Units 13 and 14 were both enriched by the storytelling of Bailey Phelps, a tribal member of the Cherokee Nation. Bailey Phelps shares his love of heritage and cultural history through storytelling at festivals and schools. He has published four books, including *They Loved the Land* and *With Our Own Eyes*.

Our deepest appreciation to Bailey for sharing his storytelling with us.

New and Important Objectives
A Research-Based Reading Program

Phonemic Awareness
Phonics
Fluency
Vocabulary
Comprehension

Phonological and Phonemic Awareness
Blending; Rhyming; Onset and Rime; Counting Syllables

Phonics
Cumulative Letter Sounds and Combinations
Review • Ss, Ee, ee, Mm, Aa, Dd, th, Nn, Tt, Ww, Ii, Th, Hh, Cc, Rr, ea, sh, Sh, Kk, -ck, oo, ar, wh, Wh, ĕ, -y (as in fly), Ll, Oo, Bb, all, Gg, Ff, Uu, er, oo (as in book), Yy, a (schwa), Pp, ay, Vv, Qq, Jj, Xx, or, Zz, a_e, -y (as in baby), i_e, ou, ow (as in cow), ch, Ch, ai, igh, o_e, ir, aw, ew, ue, u_e, ow (as in snow), ge, -dge, ci, ce, kn, ph, oa, oi, ea (as in bread), gi, au, oy

Cumulative Affixes, Morphographs, and Open Syllables
Review • -ed, -en, -er, -es, -est, -ing, -ly, -s, -y, -tion, re-, un-, ex-, o (as in open), -ful, bi-, de-, -able, i (as in silence), be-, -ous, dis-

★New Letter Sounds, Combinations, Affixes, and Morphographs
-al (as in animal) • coastal, dental, nocturnal, numeral
-ible (as in flexible) • collectible, incredible, susceptible, visible

★New Proper Nouns
Ann's, Central America, Lion, Raven, Southeast Asia's, Texas, Thailand

★New Pattern Words
barn, barns, beck, birth, bleed, blind, bounce, bounces, brave, buck, bulge, cawed, chill, else, fooled, fuss, grace, honk, honked, laps, less, owl, owls, peach, peak, rate, ripe, roost, roosts, shrink, shrinking, sloths, slots, snap, snapped, snout, snug, strut, strutted, teak, trout, whirl

* **Known Pattern Words With Affixes, Known Tricky Words With Affixes,** and **Known Multisyllabic Words With Affixes** have base words students have previously read. The words are new in this unit because they have not been previously read with the affix.

★ = New in this unit

Phonics (continued)

*Known Pattern Words With Affixes • based, breathing, creepy, cupful, drinks, facing, fighting, hangs, hatched, hiding, howled, moths, scary, screeching, slows, snakes, tiredly, unknowing

★New Compound and Hyphenated Words

bat-like, cape-like, catfish, daytime, echolocation, farmland, grasshoppers, hand-like, hand-wings, newborn, pig-like, sleep-like, somewhere, tailbone, teaspoons, upside, wingspan

★Other New Multisyllabic Words

active, approaches, bewitching, billow, billowy, bumblebee, classify, common, company, compared, endangered, extinction, fabric, hibernate, hibernation, hollow, importance, impressive, jacket, jackets, location, migrate, obvious, obviously, ostriches, pandas, penny, pigeon, polar, pollen, pollinate, pollinating, populations, powder, regions, relate, related, remarkable, repeats, return, scorpion, scorpions, shallow, spindly, successful, summary, superb, upper, vampire, weather, yippee

*Known Multisyllabic Words With Affixes • beetles, belly's, continues, fluttered, legends, mosquitoes, predators, studying

★New Tricky Words

blood, characteristics, chief, echo, lose, losing, machine, machines, salmon, suited, whistle

*Known Tricky Words With Affixes • becomes, breaking, groups, juicy, unusual, warmer, wasps

Fluency

Accuracy, Expression, Phrasing, Rate

Vocabulary

New • billow, characteristics, classify, common, echo, endangered, flexible, location, mammal, nocturnal, obvious, obviously, pollen, prey, roost

Review • allow, amazing, carnivore, colony, congratulate, creature, curious, dangerous, destroy, endangered, except, extinct, habitat, herbivore, hesitate, insist, legend, life cycle, locate, obey, ordinary, predator, protect, summon, treasure, trickster, valuable, weary

Reviewed in Context • allow, amazed, amazing, carnivore, colony, creature, except, extinct, fascinated, generation, habit, habitat, herbivore, legend, locate, ordinary, planet, predator, pretend, realize, reptile, senses, surface, survive, trickster

Comprehension

Unit Genres

Nonfiction • Expository

Poetry • Narrative

Comprehension Processes

Build Knowledge: Factual, Procedural, Conceptual

Day	1	2	3	4	5	6
Remember						
Defining					E	
Identifying (recalling)	S,C	S,C	S,C	S,C	S,C	C
Using				S		
Understand						
Defining (in your own words)	S,C		S	S,C	E,C	
Describing				S,C	S	
Explaining (rephrasing)	S	S	S	S	S	
Illustrating	C	C				
Sequencing				C		C
Summarizing			E	S	S,C	
Using	S,C	S,C	S	C	E,S	C
Visualizing	C	C		S		
Apply						
Demonstrating				S		
Explaining (unstated)	S		S	S	S	
Illustrating	C	C				
Inferring	S	S	S	S,C	S	C
Making Connections (relating)	S			S		
Predicting	S,C	S				
Using			S	S	S	
Analyze						
Classifying			E,S,C		S	
Comparing/Contrasting	S	S,C		S		
Distinguishing Cause/Effect						
Drawing Conclusions		S		S	S	
Inferring			S			
Evaluate						
Making Judgments						
Responding (personal)	S					
Create						
Generating Ideas			S	S,C	E,S	

E = Exercise, S = Storybook, C = Comprehension & Skill

Comprehension (continued)

Skills and Strategies

Day	1	2	3	4	5	6
Priming Background Knowledge	S		S	S		
Setting a Purpose for Reading	S			S		
Answering Questions	S	S	S	S,C	S	S
Asking Questions			S	S	S	
Visualizing	C	C		S		
Comprehension Monitoring/Fix Ups						
Does it Make Sense?		C		C	E,C	
Looking Back						
Restating						
Summarizing						
Main Idea					C	
Retelling						
Supporting Details					C	
Understanding Text Structure						
Title, Author, Illustrator	S	S	S	S	S	
Fact or Fiction						
Genre (Classifying)	S					
Narrative						
Setting	S,C	S,C				
Main Character/Traits (Characterization)*	S	S				
Goal	S					
Problem/Solution	S,C	S,C				
Action/Events/Sequence	S	S				
Outcome/Conclusion		S,C				
Lesson/Author's Message		S,C				
Expository						
Subject/Topic			C	C	E,C	C
Heading					S	
Supporting Details (Facts/Information)			C	S,C	E,S,C	C
Main Idea			C	C		C
Using Graphic Organizers						
Chart						
Diagram (labeling)				C		
Hierarchy (topic/detail)			E,S,C	C	C	
K-W-L			S		S	
Map (locating, labeling)						
Matrix (compare/contrast)		S,C				
Sequence (linear, cycle, cause and effect)						
Story Map						
Web						

E = Exercise, S = Storybook, C = Comprehension & Skill

* Narrator

Comprehension (continued)

Study Skills

Day	1	2	3	4	5	6
Alphabetical Order	C					
Following Directions						
Locating Information	C		S	C	S,C	
Note Taking						C
Previewing						
Reviewing		S		S	S	
Test Taking						C
Using Glossary	S		S			
Using Table of Contents	S					
Viewing	S		S	C		
Verifying					S	

Writing in Response to Reading

Day	1	2	3	4	5	6
Sentence Completion	C	C	C	C	C	C
Making Lists						
Sentence Writing				C		
Story Retell/Summary						
Fact Summary			C		C	
Paragraph Writing				C	C	
Report Writing						
Open-Ended Response						
Creative Writing						

Writing Traits

(Addressed within the context of Writing in Response to Reading)

Day	1	2	3	4	5	6
Ideas and Content						
Elaborating/Generating					C	
Organization						
Introduction						
Topic Sentence					C	
Supporting Details					C	
Sequencing				C		
Word Choice						
Sophisticated Words (Tier 2 and 3)					E,C	
Conventions						
Capital	C			C	C	C
Ending Punctuation	C	C	C	C	C	C
Other (commas, quotation marks)	C					
Presentation						
Handwriting	C				C	C
Neatness	C				C	C

E = Exercise, S = Storybook, C = Comprehension & Skill

Daily Lesson Planning

LESSON PLAN FORMAT

Teacher-Directed 45 Minutes		Independent Teacher-Directed, as needed
Lesson Part 1 (Phonological Awareness, Phonics, Fluency, Comprehension) 15–20 Minutes	**Lesson Part 2** (Vocabulary, Fluency, Comprehension) 20–25 Minutes	**Lesson Part 3** (Vocabulary, Fluency, Comprehension) 15–20 Minutes
• Exercises	• Unit and/or Story Opener • Vocabulary • Interactive Story Reading • Short Passage Practice Timed Readings	• Story Reading With Partner or Whisper Reading • Comprehension and Skill Activities

HOMEWORK

Read Well Homework (blackline masters of new *Read Well 2* passages) provides an opportunity for children to celebrate accomplishments with parents. Homework should be sent home on routine days.

ORAL READING FLUENCY ASSESSMENT

Upon completion of this unit, assess each student and proceed to Unit 15, as appropriate.

WRITTEN ASSESSMENT

During the time students would normally complete Comprehension and Skill Activities, students will be administered a Written Assessment that can be found on page 103 in the students' *Activity Book 3*.

Note: See Making Decisions for additional assessment information.

DIFFERENTIATED LESSON PLANS

The differentiated lesson plans illustrate how to use materials for students with various learning needs. As you set up your unit plan, always include *Read Well 2* Exercises and Story Reading on a daily basis. Unit 14 includes 6-, 8-, 9-, 10-, and 11-Day Plans.

Plans	For groups that:
6-DAY	Complete Oral Reading Fluency Assessments with Passes and Strong Passes
8-DAY	Complete Oral Reading Fluency Assessments with Passes and require teacher-guided assistance with Story Reading and Comprehension and Skill Work
9-, 10-, or 11-DAY	Have difficulty passing the unit Oral Reading Fluency Assessments

6-DAY PLAN

Day 1	Day 2	Day 3
Teacher-Directed • Exercise 1 • Unit and Story Opener: The War Between Birds and Mammals • Vocabulary, Intro, Ch. 1, 2 • The War Between Birds and Mammals, Intro, Ch. 1 • Guide practice, as needed, on Comp & Skill 1, 2 **Independent Work** • On Your Own: Partner or Whisper Read, The War Between Birds and Mammals, Ch. 2 • Comp & Skill 1, 2 **Homework** • Homework Passage 1	**Teacher-Directed** • Exercise 2 • The War Between Birds and Mammals, Ch. 3 • Story Comparison: Focus Lesson • Guide practice, as needed, on Comp & Skill 3, 4 **Independent Work** • Repeated Reading: Partner or Whisper Read, The War Between Birds and Mammals, Ch. 3 • Comp & Skill 3, 4 **Homework** • Homework Passage 2	**Teacher-Directed** • Exercise 3a • Exercise 3b: Focus Lesson • Story Opener: Incredible Flying Machine • K-W-L (modified) • Vocabulary, Ch. 1 • Incredible Flying Machine, Ch. 1 • Guide practice, as needed, on Comp & Skill Classification Chart **Independent Work** • Repeated Reading: Partner or Whisper Read, Incredible Flying Machine, Ch. 1 • Comp & Skill Classification Chart **Homework** • Homework Passage 3
Day 4	**Day 5**	**Day 6**
Teacher-Directed • Exercise 4 • Vocabulary, Ch. 2, 3 • Incredible Flying Machine, Ch. 2 • Guide practice, as needed, on Comp & Skill 5, 6 **Independent Work** • On Your Own: Partner or Whisper Read, Incredible Flying Machine, Ch. 3 • Comp & Skill 5, 6 **Homework** • Homework Passage 4	**Teacher-Directed** • Exercise 5a • Exercise 5b: Focus Lesson • Vocabulary, Ch. 4 • Incredible Flying Machine, Ch. 4 • K-W-L (modified) • Guide practice, as needed, on Comp & Skill 7, 8 **Independent Work** • Repeated Reading: Partner or Whisper Read, Incredible Flying Machine, Ch. 4 • Comp & Skill 7, 8 **Homework** • Homework Passage 5	**Teacher-Directed** • Exercise 6 • Fluency, A Bat's Life **Independent Work** • Repeated Reading: Partner or Whisper Read, A Bat's Life • Written Assessment • Oral Reading Fluency Assessment* **Homework** • Homework Passage 6

Note: Unit 14 features an extra Just for Fun Comp & Skill activity, located after Activity 4. This page can be used any time during the unit. The Just for Fun activity allows the related activities, story map and written retell, to be located side by side in the Activity Book.

* The Oral Reading Fluency Assessments are individually administered by the teacher while students are working on their Written Assessments.

8-DAY PLAN • *Pre-Intervention*

Day 1

Teacher-Directed
- Exercise 1
- Unit and Story Opener: The War Between Birds and Mammals
- Vocabulary, Intro, Ch. 1, 2
- The War Between Birds and Mammals, Intro, Ch. 1
- Guide practice, Comp & Skill 1

Independent Work
- Repeated Reading: Partner or Whisper Read, The War Between Birds and Mammals, Intro, Ch. 1
- Comp & Skill 1

Homework
- Extra Practice Word Fluency A

Day 2

Teacher-Directed
- Review Exercise 1
- Review Vocabulary, Intro, Ch. 1, 2
- The War Between Birds and Mammals, Ch. 2
- Guide practice, as needed, on Comp & Skill 2

Independent Work
- Repeated Reading: Partner or Whisper Read, The War Between Birds and Mammals, Ch. 2
- Comp & Skill 2

Homework
- Homework Passage 1

Day 3

Teacher-Directed
- Exercise 2
- The War Between Birds and Mammals, Ch. 3
- Story Comparison: Focus Lesson
- Guide practice, as needed, on Comp & Skill 3, 4

Independent Work
- Repeated Reading: Partner or Whisper Read, The War Between Birds and Mammals, Ch. 3
- Comp & Skill 3, 4

Homework
- Homework Passage 2

Day 4

Teacher-Directed
- Exercise 3a
- Exercise 3b: Focus . . .
- Story Opener: Incredible Flying Machine
- K-W-L (modified)
- Vocabulary, Ch. 1
- Incredible Flying Machine, Ch. 1
- Guide practice, Comp & Skill Classification Chart

Independent Work
- Repeated Reading: Partner or Whisper Read, Incredible Flying Machine, Ch. 1
- Comp & Skill Classification Chart

Homework
- Homework Passage 3

Day 5

Teacher-Directed
- Exercise 4
- Vocabulary, Ch. 2, 3
- Incredible Flying Machine, Ch. 2
- Guide practice, as needed, on Comp & Skill 5

Independent Work
- Repeated Reading: Partner or Whisper Read, Incredible Flying Machine, Ch. 2
- Comp & Skill 5

Homework
- Homework Passage 4

Day 6

Teacher-Directed
- Review Exercise 4
- Review Vocabulary, Ch. 2, 3
- Incredible Flying Machine, Ch. 3
- Guide practice, as needed, on Comp & Skill 6

Independent Work
- Repeated Reading: Partner or Whisper Read, Incredible Flying Machine, Ch. 3
- Comp & Skill 6

Homework
- Homework Passage 5

Day 7

Teacher-Directed
- Exercise 5a
- Exercise 5b: Focus . . .
- Vocabulary, Ch. 4
- Incredible Flying Machine, Ch. 4
- K-W-L (modified)
- Guide practice, Comp & Skill 7, 8

Independent Work
- Repeated Reading: Partner or Whisper Read, Incredible Flying Machine, Ch. 4
- Comp & Skill 7, 8

Homework
- Comp & Skill 7 (Fluency)

Day 8

Teacher-Directed
- Exercise 6
- Fluency, A Bat's Life

Independent Work
- Repeated Reading: Partner or Whisper Read, A Bat's Life
- Written Assessment
- Oral Reading Fluency Assessment*

Homework
- Homework Passage 6

9-, 10-, or 11-DAY PLAN • *Intervention*
For Days 1–8, follow 8-Day plan. Add Days 9, 10, 11 as follows:

Day 9 Extra Practice 1

Teacher-Directed
- Decoding Practice
- Fluency Passage

Independent Work
- Activity and Word Fluency A

Homework
- Fluency Passage

Day 10 Extra Practice 2

Teacher-Directed
- Decoding Practice
- Fluency Passage

Independent Work
- Activity and Word Fluency B

Homework
- Fluency Passage

Day 11 Extra Practice 3

Teacher-Directed
- Decoding Practice
- Fluency Passage

Independent Work
- Activity and Word Fluency A or B
- ORF Assessment*

Homework
- Fluency Passage

Materials and Materials Preparation

Core Lessons

Teacher Materials

READ WELL 2 MATERIALS

- Unit 14 Teacher's Guide
- Sound Cards
- Unit 14 Oral Reading Fluency Assessment found on page 104
- Group Assessment Record found in the *Assessment Manual*

SCHOOL SUPPLIES

Stopwatch or watch with a second hand

Student Materials

READ WELL 2 MATERIALS (for each student)

- *Spiders and Bats* storybook
- *Exercise Book 3*
- *Activity Book 3* or copies of Unit 14 Comprehension and Skill Work
- Unit 14 Written Assessment found in *Activity Book 3*, page 103, and on the blackline master CD
- Unit 14 Certificate of Achievement (BLM, page 105)
- Unit 14 Homework (blackline masters)
  See *Getting Started* for suggested homework routines.

SCHOOL SUPPLIES

Pencils, colors (optional—markers, crayons, or colored pencils)

> Make one copy per student of each blackline master, as appropriate for the group.
>
> *Note:* For new or difficult Comprehension and Skill Activities, make overhead transparencies from the blackline masters. Use the transparencies to demonstrate and guide practice.

Extra Practice Lessons

> **CAUTION**
> Use these lessons only if needed. Students who need Extra Practice may benefit from one, two, or three lessons.

Student Materials

READ WELL 2 MATERIALS (for each student, as needed)

See Extra Practice blackline masters.

- Unit 14 Extra Practice 1: Decoding Practice, Fluency Passage, Word Fluency A, and Activity
- Unit 14 Extra Practice 2: Decoding Practice, Fluency Passage, Word Fluency B, and Activity
- Unit 14 Extra Practice 3: Decoding Practice, Fluency Passage, Word Fluency A or B, and Activity

SCHOOL SUPPLIES

Pencils, colors (markers, crayons, or colored pencils), highlighters

> **CLASSIFICATION CHART**
> Your students will complete a classification chart and fact summary. For ease of use, pull pages 19–22 from *Activity Book 3*, and staple them together.

> **FOCUS LESSONS**
> For Exercises 3b and 5b (Focus Lessons), make overhead transparencies from the blackline masters, write on transparencies placed over the pages, or use paper copies to demonstrate how to complete the lessons.

Important Tips

A Letter to the Kids from the *Read Well* Authors
Working with English Language Learners

A Letter to the Kids from the Read Well Authors

Send student letters to: *Read Well* Authors, P.O. Box 50550, Eugene, OR 97405. If you wish to receive a return note, include a postage-paid, self-addressed envelope and a short description of your students (grade level and demographics). We would love to hear from you as well.

> Dear Kids:
>
> We hope you are having fun with *Read Well 2*. You've read stories about Africa, Hawaii, animal colonies, and tsunamis. You've read new stories and old stories. You've read fiction and nonfiction. You can read and understand a lot of sophisticated words like cephalothorax, determined, and fascinated. You've even written your own report. We think you are scholars!
>
> We hope you'll write to us. We'd love to hear:
> —something about you
> —what your favorite *Read Well* story is so far and why
> —what you'd like to read about next
>
> We'll write you back! Hope to hear from you soon.
>
> > Sincerely,
> > *Read Well* 2 Authors
> > (Mrs. Sprick, Ms. Watanabe, Mrs. Akiyama-Paik, and Mrs. Jones)

Working with English Language Learners

WHAT RESEARCH SUGGESTS

The National Center for Education Evaluation and Regional Assistance (2007) recommends that ELLs receive instruction in phonemic awareness, phonics, vocabulary, comprehension, and fluency. When English Language Learners (ELLs) are placed appropriately in *Read Well*, they receive instruction that aligns with research-based recommendations for ELLs. The committee also suggests that instruction should be delivered, along with formative assessments, through focused and intensive small group intervention with vocabulary instruction throughout the day, peer-assisted learning, and the development of academic English.

INTENSIVE SMALL GROUP INTERVENTION

When ELLs receive a second dose of *Read Well* instruction each day, learning can be enhanced. If you aren't doing so already, provide ELLs with a second dose of *Read Well* instruction.

HOW TO ENHANCE VOCABULARY INSTRUCTION AND THE DEVELOPMENT OF ACADEMIC LANGUAGE

In the second dose of *Read Well* instruction, instructors can:

- Preteach common words that are central to understanding the story.

  For example, for Unit 14, Chapter 1 of "Incredible Flying Machines," an ELL teacher might preteach the common word "group," which is central to the content of Chapter 1. The teacher could point to the pictures on storybook pages 80 and 81 and say something like:
  This is a *group* of animals called . . . fish.
  This is a group of animals called . . . arachnids.
  This is a group of animals called . . . birds.
  Say the next sentence with me. This is a group of animals called mammals.

- Preteach *selected Read Well* vocabulary using the storybook vocabulary pages, additional pictures, and artifacts.

  The ELL teacher may also preteach the *Read Well* vocabulary word "classify" because it is central to the content of Chapter 1. The ELL teacher might pass out a blank flowchart and pictures of animals to partners. Then say something like:
  Touch the *group* of animals called fish. Put the fish pictures under the word *fish*. You just *classified* three fish. What did you do? Classified the fish.
  The word *classified* is a snazzy word. Say the word. (classified)
  Now put the bee, ant, and grasshopper on the chart where they belong.
  What group do they belong in? (insects) You classified the insects.
  What did you do? (classified the insects) Yes, you classified the insects.
  Say the whole sentence. We classified the insects.

- Read the next day's story or selected portions of the story to students while they finger track. Have students answer questions using Partner Think and Talk procedures. Paraphrase student answers using complete sentences, appropriate syntax, and word choice, then have students repeat back.
- Preview and orally discuss the next day's written Comprehension and Skill Work.

How to Teach the Lessons

Teach from this section. Each instructional component is outlined in an easy-to-teach format.

Exercise 1

- Unit and Story Opener: Bats,
  The War Between Birds and Mammals
- Vocabulary
- Story Reading 1
  With the Teacher: Introduction, Chapter 1
  On Your Own: Chapter 2
- Comprehension and Skill Activities 1, 2

Exercise 2

- Story Reading 2
  With the Teacher: Chapter 3
- Story Comparison: Focus Lesson
- Comprehension and Skill Activities 3, 4

Exercise 3a

- Exercise 3b: Focus Lesson
- Story Opener: Incredible Flying Machine
- Vocabulary
- Story Reading 3
  With the Teacher: Chapter 1
- Comprehension and Skill Classification Chart

Exercise 4

- Vocabulary
- Story Reading 4
  With the Teacher: Chapter 2
  On Your Own: Chapter 3
- Comprehension and Skill Activities 5, 6

Exercise 5a

- Exercise 5b: Focus Lesson
- Vocabulary
- Story Reading 5
  With the Teacher: Chapter 4
- Comprehension and Skill Activities 7, 8

Exercise 6

- Story Reading 6
  With the Teacher: A Bat's Life (Fluency)
- Written Assessment

Note: Lessons include daily homework.

① SOUND REVIEW
Use selected Sound Cards from Units 1–13.

PACING
Exercise 1 should take
about 15 minutes.

② SOUND PRACTICE
- For each task, have students spell and say the focus sound in the gray bar.
  Next, have students read each underlined sound, the word, then the whole column.
- Repeat with each column, building accuracy first, then fluency.

③ ACCURACY AND FLUENCY BUILDING
- For each task, have students say any underlined part, then read the word.
- Set a pace. Then have students read the whole words in each task and column.
- Provide repeated practice, building accuracy first, then fluency.

C1. Multisyllabic Words
- For the list of words divided by syllables, have students read each syllable, then the whole word. Use the word in a sentence, as appropriate.
- For the list of whole words, build accuracy and then fluency

yippee	When Aisha won the race, she said . . . *"Yippee."*
reason	When the teacher asked Kat why she was late, she didn't have a . . . *reason.*
trickster	A character in a story who tricks or cheats others is called a . . . *trickster.*
continues	Alvin hasn't stopped reading. He . . . *continues* . . . to read.
introduction	Sometimes the author introduces us to the story's characters in the . . . *introduction.*
somewhere	Josh just knew he left his bike . . . *somewhere.*

D1. Tricky Words
- For each Tricky Word, have students use the sounds and word parts they know to silently sound out the word. Use the word in a sentence to help with pronunciation.
- If the word is unfamiliar, tell students the word.

chief
Look at the first word. Sound the word out silently. Thumbs up when you know the word. Use my sentence to help you pronounce the word. The leader of the police department is the . . . chief. Read the word three times. (chief, chief, chief)

wolf	Who's afraid of the big bad . . . *wolf?*
groups	During reading, students in our class are divided into three . . . *groups.*
against	Our soccer team will play . . . *against* . . . your team.
watched	There was a show about endangered birds on TV. We all . . . *watched* . . . it.

- Have students go back and read the whole words in the column.

★④ ANIMAL NAMES
- Tell students these are the names of animals they will read about in the story.
- Have students use the sounds and word parts they know to figure out the words. Use the words in sentences, as needed.

⑤ WORDS IN CONTEXT
For each word, have students use the sounds and word parts they know to silently sound out the word. Then have students read the sentence. Assist, as needed.

★ = New in this unit

⑥ **AFFIXES**

★Have students practice reading -*al* and the related words. Use each word in a sentence.

The War Between Birds and Mammals

Unit 14 Exercise 1
Use before the Introduction and Chapters 1 and 2

1. SOUND REVIEW Use selected Sound Cards from Units 1–13.

2. SOUND PRACTICE In each column, have students spell and say the sound, next say any underlined sound and the word, then read the column.

ow as in snow	ce	aw	u	Related Words
holl<u>ow</u>	pea<u>ce</u>	c<u>aw</u>ed	dr<u>u</u>m	hid
shad<u>ow</u>	pla<u>ce</u>	cl<u>aw</u>s	f<u>u</u>ss	hide
sh<u>ow</u>ed	<u>ce</u>lebrate	h<u>aw</u>k	h<u>u</u>nt	hiding

3. ACCURACY/FLUENCY BUILDING For each column, have students say any underlined part, then read each word. Next, have them read the column.

A1 Mixed Practice	B1 Word Endings	C1 Multisyllabic Words		D1 Tricky Words
h<u>au</u>l	honk<u>ed</u>	yip•pee	yippee	chief
gra<u>ph</u>	strutt<u>ed</u>	rea•son	reason	wolf
goose	snapp<u>ed</u>	trick•ster	trickster	groups
p<u>ea</u>k	roar<u>ed</u>	con•tin•ues	continues	against
else	howl<u>ed</u>	in•tro•duc•tion	introduction	watched
f<u>ea</u>thers	screech<u>ing</u>	some•where	somewhere	

★4. ANIMAL NAMES Have students use the sounds and word parts they know to figure out each word.

Raven	Four-Footed Ones	Mountain Lion	Winged Ones

5. WORDS IN CONTEXT Have students use the sounds and word parts they know to figure out each word. Then have them read each sentence.

Ⓐ an•gry   The <u>angry</u> birds were at war and started to fight.

Ⓑ le•gends   We love to listen to <u>legends</u> told by our grandfather.

6. AFFIXES Have students practice reading "-al" and the related words.

★-al	anim<u>al</u>	fiction<u>al</u>	mamm<u>al</u>	coast<u>al</u>

14

TEAM EXPECTATIONS
(Reminder)

Provide a quick review of expectations before starting the lesson.

1. Sit up.
2. Follow directions.
3. Help each other.
4. Work hard and have fun.

ACKNOWLEDGE STUDENTS WHEN THEY MEET YOUR EXPECTATIONS

Students respond positively when you acknowledge their accomplishments. Pair descriptive praise with an individual turn or job. [Gloria], great job sitting up and finger tracking. You have a professional attitude about your learning. Everyone, watch how [Gloria] is able to follow along while I read.

BUILD ACCURACY AND FLUENCY
(Reminder)

For all rows and columns, follow the specific directions, then build accuracy and fluency with whole words.

COMPREHENSION PROCESSES

Remember, Understand, Apply, Analyze

PROCEDURES

1. Introducing the Unit

Responding; Comparing/Contrasting; Priming Background Knowledge; Using Vocabulary—ordinary, amazing

In the last unit, we studied spiders.
Before you started the unit, what did you think about spiders?
(I thought they were ordinary. I thought they were creepy . . .)

By the time we finished the unit, what did you think?
(I decided that spiders were awesome. I learned that they are amazing builders . . .)

In this unit, we're going to study bats.
What do you think about bats now?
I wonder how you'll feel when we finish.

2. Introducing the Story

**Using Table of Contents;
Identifying—Title, Genre;
Inferring—Main Characters;
Priming Background Knowledge;
Using Vocabulary—legend**

Have students find the Table of Contents for Unit 14.
Say something like:
Everyone, find page 4 of the Table of Contents. What's the title of the first story in this unit? (The War Between Birds and Mammals)

What kind of story is it?
(fiction, legend)
Yes, this is another American Indian legend.

Who do you think the main characters in this story are?
(birds and mammals . . .)

I wonder if a bat is a bird or a mammal. Raise your hand if you think a bat is a bird. Why do you think a bat is a bird? (It flies . . .)

Raise your hand if you think a bat is a mammal. Why do you think a bat is a mammal? (It looks like a mouse . . .)

TABLE OF CONTENTS

UNIT 14 • Bats

4

3. **Introducing the Genre—
   Expository**

   **Identifying—Genre;
   Making Connections**

   The second story in this unit is
   the "Incredible Flying Machine."
   What kind of story is it?
   (nonfiction, expository)

   Expository writing is nonfiction. Was
   your spider report nonfiction? (yes)
   Expository writing also provides
   information. Did your report provide
   information about spiders? (yes)
   So, your spider report
   was . . . expository.

   I like expository writing. Maybe we'll
   find out whether a bat is a mammal
   or a bird in the expository selection.

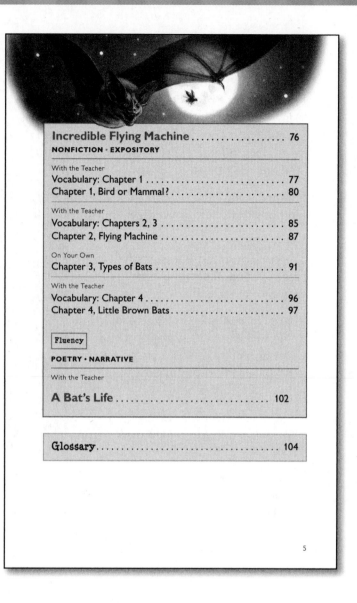

5

4. Introducing the Title Page

Identifying—Title, Author; Inferring; Priming Background Knowledge; Predicting

Have students look at the title page:

Everyone, turn to pages 60 and 61. What's the title of this story? (The War Between Birds and Mammals)

Who is this story by? (Bailey Phelps)

Bailey Phelps is an American Indian storyteller. He wrote the legend about Centipede and Grandmother Spider.

Bailey Phelps is a Cherokee tribal member. When he was growing up, who do you think told him legends? (his father, his grandfather . . .)

I think you will enjoy this story. It starts with Gray Cloud and his grandfather. What do you think Gray Cloud will do? (He will ask many questions.)

Yes, and Gray Cloud's questions will get Grandfather to tell him a story.

18

COMPREHENSION PROCESSES

Understand

PROCEDURES

1. Introducing Vocabulary

legend, trickster

- For each vocabulary word, have students read the word by parts, then read the whole word.
- Read the student-friendly explanations to students as they follow with their fingers. Then have students use the vocabulary word by following the gray text.
- Review and discuss the photos and illustrations.

2. Now You Try It!

- Read or paraphrase the directions.
- Have students read the word by parts, then read the whole word.
- Have students explain or define the word in their own words.
- Have students turn to the appropriate page in the glossary and discuss how their definition is the same as or different from the glossary's. Your students may like their definition better.

Note: By defining a word in their own words, students are demonstrating depth of word knowledge. Verbatim responses only demonstrate memorization. Encourage paraphrasing.

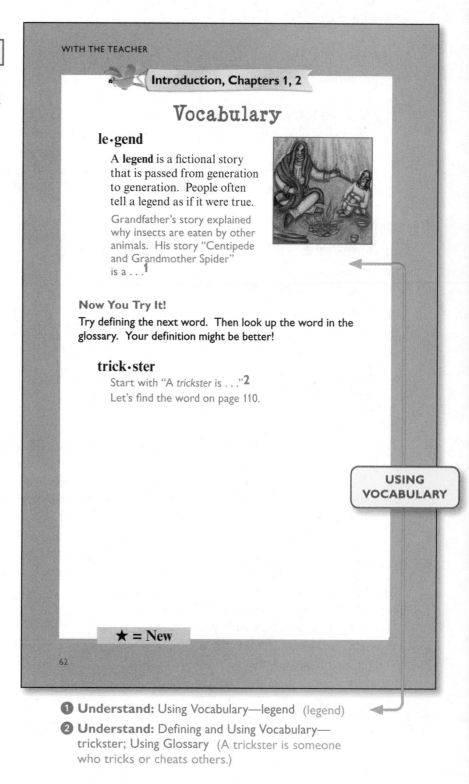

WITH THE TEACHER

Introduction, Chapters 1, 2

Vocabulary

le·gend

A **legend** is a fictional story that is passed from generation to generation. People often tell a legend as if it were true.

Grandfather's story explained why insects are eaten by other animals. His story "Centipede and Grandmother Spider" is a . . .[1]

Now You Try It!

Try defining the next word. Then look up the word in the glossary. Your definition might be better!

trick·ster

Start with "A *trickster* is . . ."[2]
Let's find the word on page 110.

USING VOCABULARY

★ = New

62

❶ **Understand:** Using Vocabulary—legend (legend)
❷ **Understand:** Defining and Using Vocabulary— trickster; Using Glossary (A trickster is someone who tricks or cheats others.)

CHAPTER 1 INSTRUCTIONS

Students read the Introduction and Chapter 1 with the teacher and Chapter 2 on their own.

Note: If you're working on an 8- to 11-Day Plan, you will read Chapter 2 with students.

COMPREHENSION PROCESSES

Remember, Understand, Apply

COMPREHENSION BUILDING

- Encourage students to answer questions with complete sentences, when appropriate.
- If students have difficulty comprehending, think aloud with them or reread the portion of the story that answers the question. Repeat the question.

PROCEDURES

1. Introducing the Introduction and Chapter 1

Identifying—What

Say something like:

Turn to page 63. This part of the story is called the . . . (Introduction).

In this introduction, Bailey Phelps introduces us to the legend that Grandfather will tell to Gray Cloud.

The first chapter of this story is the beginning of the legend, "The War Between Birds and Mammals."

> **CORRECTING DECODING ERRORS**
>
> During story reading, gently correct any error, then have students reread the sentence.

2. First Reading

- Ask questions and discuss the text as indicated by the gray text.
- Mix group and individual turns, independent of your voice. Have students work toward a group accuracy goal of 0–6 errors. Quietly keep track of errors made by all students in the group.
- After reading the story, practice any difficult words. Repeat, if students have not reached the accuracy goal.

3. Second Reading, Short Passage Practice: Developing Prosody

- Demonstrate expressive, fluent reading of the first paragraph. Read at a rate slightly faster than the students' rate.
- Guide practice with your voice.
- Provide individual turns while others track with their fingers and whisper read.
- Repeat with one paragraph at a time.

> **REPEATED READINGS**
>
> **Prosody**
>
> On the second reading, students practice developing prosody— phrasing and expression. Research has shown that prosody is related to both fluency and comprehension.

THE WAR BETWEEN BIRDS AND MAMMALS

Introduction

The little boy's name was Gray Cloud. He sat on a smooth rock high in the hills with his grandfather.

The sun was setting behind the mountains. The dark shadow of the peak reached out to cover the man and the little boy.

Something flew by. It was a bat. "Grandfather," said Gray Cloud, "why do bats fly so fast?"

"They are hungry," said Grandfather. "They catch insects right out of the air."

"Is the cave their home?" asked the boy.

Grandfather said, "Yes. At night they come out and hunt for food."

Gray Cloud asked, "Why do bats hunt only at night?"

Grandfather had been waiting for this question. He said, "I can tell you how this came to be. You must listen with both ears at once."

What questions do you think this *legend* will answer?**1** Why did Grandfather tell Gray Cloud to listen with both ears?**2**

63

COMPREHENDING AS YOU GO

1 **Apply:** Predicting; Using Vocabulary—legend (It will tell us why bats fly so fast and why they hunt only at night.)

2 **Apply:** Inferring, Explaining (He wants Gray Cloud to pay close attention.)

WITH THE TEACHER

64

FOCUS ON VIEWING

Identifying—Who, Setting; Inferring

Look at the picture. Who is in the picture? (Gray Cloud and his Grandfather) When do you think Grandfather told this story to Gray Cloud? (long ago) What makes you think this? (There are tepees.)

THE WAR BETWEEN BIRDS AND MAMMALS

Chapter 1

The Birds and Mammals Get Angry

A long time ago, back in the beginning, the Winged Ones and the Four-Footed Ones lived together in a big forest. Eagle was chief of the birds, the Winged Ones. Bear was chief of the mammals, the Four-Footed Ones. For a long time, they were at peace. Then, for some reason that no one can remember, they began to fuss with each other.

Eagle came to Bear and said, "From now on, the forest belongs to the Winged Ones. You Four-Foots must leave."

Bear said, "No, not us. You Winged Ones must leave. The forest is ours. You go somewhere else."

Who are the Winged Ones?[1] Who are the Four-Footed Ones?[2] What is their problem?[3] What does each group want?[4]

65

COMPREHENDING AS YOU GO

❶ Apply: Inferring—Who (The Winged Ones are the birds.)

❷ Apply: Inferring—Who (The Four-Footed Ones are the mammals.)

❸ Understand: Explaining—Problem (They are fussing with each other.)

❹ Understand: Explaining—Goal (Each group wants the other to leave the forest.)

WITH THE TEACHER

The two groups began a war. Bear waved his huge paws at the birds. Wolf leaped and snapped at the birds. Bear roared. Wolf howled, and Mountain Lion growled.

All during the war, Bat hid inside a hollow tree. He watched and stayed quiet.

At the end of the day, the mammals won, so they made the birds leave the forest. The mammals held a big party to celebrate. Bat came out of his hiding place. He strutted around, saying, "Oh boy, we won! Yippee! Let's eat."

Bear looked at Bat and said, "I did not see you in the war. Are you one of us?"

Bat kept his wings tight against his body and showed his sharp little teeth. "I'm one of you," he said. "I have teeth, see? Birds don't have teeth. I have fur, not feathers. I'm a Four-Foot."

Bear said, "Welcome then."

"I fooled them," thought Bat, and he ate, and ate, and ate until his little stomach was tight as a drum!

What was the problem?[1] Who hid inside a hollow tree during the fighting?[2] Who won the war?[3] What did Bat do to show Bear that he was a mammal?[4]

66

COMPREHENDING
AS YOU GO

1 Apply: Inferring—Problem (The birds and the mammals began a war.)

2 Remember: Identifying—Who (Bat hid inside the hollow tree.)

3 Remember: Identifying—Who (The mammals won the war.)

4 Understand: Explaining; **Apply:** Inferring (Bat kept his wings tight against his body and showed Bear his sharp teeth. He didn't want to show Bear his wings because Bear would think he was a bird.)

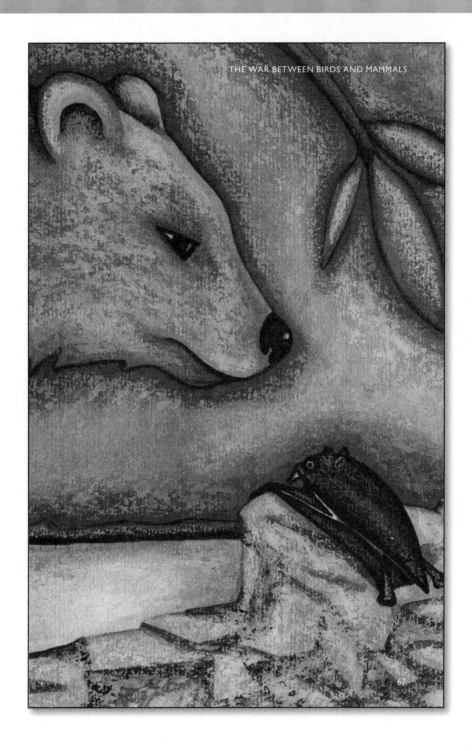

THE WAR BETWEEN BIRDS AND MAMMALS

WITH THE TEACHER

Think and Talk

PREDICTION

1. What questions will the story answer?

PROBLEM

2. What was the problem in the forest?

INFERRING

3. Who do you think is the trickster? Why?

PREDICTION

4. What do you think will happen to Bat?
Why?

68

❶ **Apply:** Predicting (The story should answer why bats fly so fast and why they fly at night.)

❷ **Apply:** Explaining—Problem (The birds wanted the forest for themselves. The mammals wanted the forest for themselves. The animals didn't want to share . . .)

❸ **Understand:** Inferring; Explaining; Using Vocabulary—trickster (Bat is the trickster. He tried to fool Bear by hiding his wings.)

❹ **Apply:** Predicting, Explaining (He will be punished for being a trickster.)

CHAPTER 2 INSTRUCTIONS

Students read without the teacher, independently or with partners.

Note: If you're working on an 8- to 11-Day Plan, you will read Chapter 2 with students.

COMPREHENSION PROCESSES

Remember, Apply, Analyze

PROCEDURES FOR READING ON YOUR OWN

1. Getting Ready

Have students turn to Chapter 2 on page 69.

2. Setting a Purpose

Identifying—Title, Who; Explaining—Action

Before students begin reading, say something like:

Read the title of this chapter. (The War Continues)

Oh dear, that means the birds and mammals must keep on fighting.

Read to find out the answers to these questions:

- What did Bat do during the next battle between the birds and the mammals?
- Who won in Chapter 2?
- How did Bat try to trick the winners?

> **PREP NOTE**
>
> **Setting a Purpose**
>
> Write questions on a chalkboard, white board, or large piece of paper before working with your small group.

3. Reading on Your Own: Partner or Whisper Reading

- Have students take turns reading every other page with a partner or have students whisper read on their own.
- Continue having students track each word with their fingers.
- Have students ask themselves or their partners the gray text questions.

For Whisper Reading, say something like:

Everyone, turn to page 69. This is where you're going to start reading on your own—without me. Please whisper read with your finger, so I can see where you are in your work.

Turn to page 70. That's where you are going to stop reading.

For Partner Reading, say something like:

Everyone, turn to page 69. This is where you're going to start Partner Reading.

Where are you going to sit? (at our desks, side by side)

You will take turns reading pages. If you are the listener, what will you do?

(keep my book flat, follow with my finger, ask the questions, compliment my partner)

If you are the reader, what will you do?

(keep my book flat, finger track, read quietly, answer the questions)

Turn to page 70. That's where you are going to stop reading.

4. Comprehension and Skill Work

For students on a 6-Day Plan, tell them they will do Comprehension and Skill Activities 1 and 2 after they read on their own. Guide practice, as needed. For teacher directions, see pages 30 and 31. (For 8- to 11-Day Plans, see the Lesson Planner, page 9.)

5. Homework 1: Repeated Reading

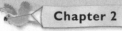

Chapter 2

The War Continues

The next day, the Winged Ones came back and began the war again. Bat hid again in his hollow tree. He watched and kept quiet.

Eagle and Hawk used their sharp claws to fight the mammals. Eagle screamed his war song. Raven cawed, and Goose honked. The air was filled with the sound of wings flapping and birds screeching.

At the end of this day, the birds won, so they made the mammals leave the forest. The birds held a big party to celebrate. Bat came out of his hiding place. He strutted around, saying, "Oh boy, we won! Yippee! Let's eat!"

Who won this time?**1** Now what do you think Bat wants to be—a bird or a mammal?**2**

69

COMPREHENDING AS YOU GO

1 **Remember:** Identifying—Who (This time the birds won.)

2 **Apply:** Inferring (Bat wants to be a bird now.)

28

ON YOUR OWN

Eagle looked at Bat and said, "I did not see you in the war. Are you one of us?"

Bat kept his mouth closed to hide his teeth. Then he showed his wings and flew up, and down, and around. "I'm one of you," he said. "Four-Foots don't have wings. They can't fly. I can fly, see?"

So Eagle said, "Welcome then."

"I fooled them all," thought Bat. He ate, and ate, and ate until his little stomach was tight as a drum!

Bat thinks he fooled the birds. What do you think will happen next?**1**

70

COMPREHENDING
AS YOU GO

1 **Apply:** Predicting, Explaining (Eagle will figure out that Bat is fooling them. Bat will be in trouble . . .)

STORY COMPREHENSION

COMPREHENSION PROCESSES

Remember, Apply

WRITING TRAITS

Conventions—Complete Sentence, Capital, Period, Question Mark, Quotation Marks

Identifying—What
Locating Information

Identifying—Setting

Identifying—Problem

Identifying—Where

Identifying—How

Predicting

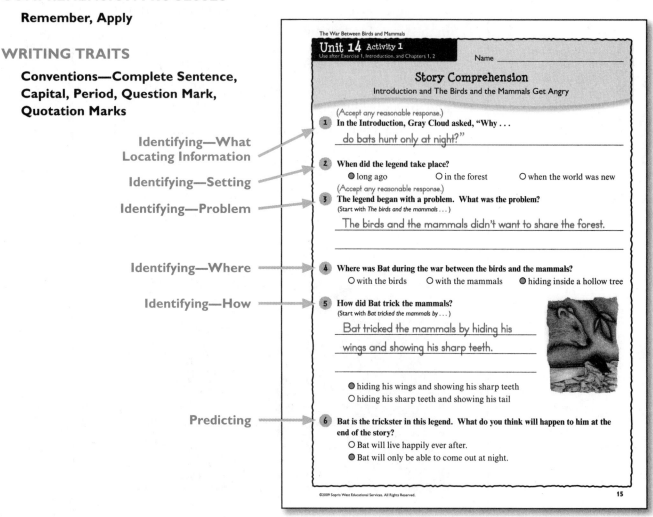

The War Between Birds and Mammals

Unit 14 Activity 1
Use after Exercise 1, Introduction, and Chapters 1, 2

Name _____

Story Comprehension
Introduction and The Birds and the Mammals Get Angry

(Accept any reasonable response.)

1. In the Introduction, Gray Cloud asked, "Why . . .
   do bats hunt only at night?"

2. When did the legend take place?
   ● long ago   ○ in the forest   ○ when the world was new

(Accept any reasonable response.)

3. The legend began with a problem. What was the problem?
   (Start with The birds and the mammals . . .)
   The birds and the mammals didn't want to share the forest.

4. Where was Bat during the war between the birds and the mammals?
   ○ with the birds   ○ with the mammals   ● hiding inside a hollow tree

5. How did Bat trick the mammals?
   (Start with Bat tricked the mammals by . . .)
   Bat tricked the mammals by hiding his
   wings and showing his sharp teeth.

   ● hiding his wings and showing his sharp teeth
   ○ hiding his sharp teeth and showing his tail

6. Bat is the trickster in this legend. What do you think will happen to him at the end of the story?
   ○ Bat will live happily ever after.
   ● Bat will only be able to come out at night.

15

PROCEDURES

For each step, demonstrate and guide practice, as needed. Then have students complete the page independently.

Selection Response—Basic Instructions (Items 1–6)

Have students read the sentence starter or questions, then fill in the bubble and/or blank with the correct answer. Remind students to start sentences with a capital and end with a period.

Note: For item 1, tell students to carefully copy the question mark and ending quotation marks from the quote in the storybook.

Self-monitoring

Have students check and correct their work.

VOCABULARY AND ALPHABETICAL ORDER

COMPREHENSION PROCESSES

Understand, Apply

WRITING TRAITS

Conventions—Complete Sentence, Capital, Period
Presentation

        Alphabetical Order

Defining and Using Vocabulary— creature; Visualizing, Illustrating

Defining and Using Vocabulary—legend

Defining and Using Vocabulary— trickster

PROCEDURES

For each step, demonstrate and guide practice, as needed. Then have students complete the page independently.

Alphabetical Order—Introductory Instructions

- Have students read the letters in the alphabet column and fill in the missing letters.
- ★Tell students they are going to find words in their storybook and write them in alphabetical order. Have students read the two examples given. Then have students select and write at least three more words from the storybook.

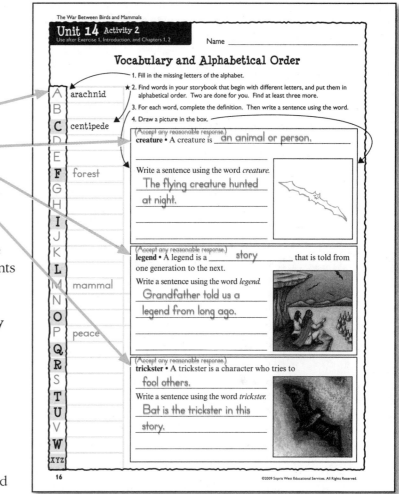

You're going to find words from your storybook and write them in alphabetical order.

Two are done for you. Read the word that is next to the letter <u>A</u>. (arachnid)

Read the word that is next to the letter <u>C</u>. (centipede)

Let's find and write another word. Look in your storybook and find a snazzy word that you would like to write on your activity page. [Marisa], what word did you find? (billowy)

What letter does *billowy* start with? (<u>b</u>) What letter will you write *billowy* next to? (<u>b</u>)

Remember, the instructions say to find *at least* three more words. Should you list two? (no)

Should you list three words? (yes) Could you list four? (yes)

That's right. *At least* three words means that you must have three, but you could have fun and list more words if you have time. There are some great snazzy words in this unit.

Vocabulary: Sentence Completion/Writing, Illustrating—Basic Instructions

- Have students read the vocabulary words.
- Have students complete the definitions by completing each sentence starter or filling in the blank.
- Have students write a sentence using each vocabulary word. Visualize and illustrate, as appropriate.

① SOUND REVIEW

Have students read the sounds and key word phrases. Work for accuracy, then fluency.

② SHIFTY WORD BLENDING

For each word, have students say the underlined sound. Then have them sound out the word smoothly and say it. Use the words in sentences, as appropriate.

③ ACCURACY AND FLUENCY BUILDING

- For each task, have students say any underlined part, then read the word.
- Set a pace. Then have students read the whole words in each task and column.
- Provide repeated practice, building accuracy first, then fluency.

A2. Rhyming Words

Have students read the words and identify what's the same about them.

B1. Bossy E

Have students identify the underlined sound and then read the word.

C1. Multisyllabic Words

- For the list of words divided by syllables, have students read each syllable, then the whole word. Use the word in a sentence, as appropriate.
- For the list of whole words, build accuracy and then fluency.

body	She lifts weights because she wants a strong . . . *body*.
during	We couldn't hear because someone was talking . . . *during* . . . the movie.
pretended	The kids played with the boxes and . . . *pretended* . . . to be robots.
moment	The store clerk said, "I'll help you in a . . . *moment*."

E1. Tricky Words

- For each Tricky Word, have students use the sounds and word parts they know to silently sound out the word. Use the word in a sentence to help with pronunciation.
- If the word is unfamiliar, tell students the word.

war	When countries fight, they are at . . . *war*.
done	I can go out and play when my homework is . . . *done*.
enough	I can't eat any more. I've had . . . *enough*.
prey	An animal that is hunted and eaten by a lion is the lion's . . . *prey*.
yourself	Please take care of . . . *yourself*.

- Have students go back and read the whole words in the column.

④ MORPHOGRAPHS AND AFFIXES

- Have students read the underlined part, then the word.
- Repeat practice with whole words, mixing group and individual turns. Build accuracy, then fluency.

⑤ GENERALIZATION: READING NEW WORDS IN PARAGRAPHS

- Have students read the paragraph silently, then out loud. Tell students to use the sounds and word parts they know to read any difficult words.
- Repeat practice, as needed.

The War Between Birds and Mammals

Unit 14 Exercise 2
Use before Chapter 3 and Story Comparison

1. SOUND REVIEW Have students review sounds for accuracy, then for fluency.

Ⓐ	ea as in bread	ci as in circle	gi as in giraffe	ge as in page	oi as in point
Ⓑ	oy	aw	kn	au	oa

2. SHIFTY WORD BLENDING For each word, have students say the underlined part, sound out smoothly, then read the word.

<u>ow</u>l	<u>grow</u>l	<u>grow</u>	grown	<u>f</u>lown

3. ACCURACY/FLUENCY BUILDING For each column, have students say any underlined part, then read each word. Next, have them read the column.

A1 Mixed Practice	**B1** Bossy <u>E</u>	**C1** Multisyllabic Words	**D1** Word Endings	**E1** Tricky Words
e<u>dge</u>	r<u>u</u>le	bod•y	<u>fight</u>ing	war
<u>new</u>	c<u>a</u>ves	dur•ing	<u>branch</u>es	done
<u>knew</u>	sh<u>a</u>re	pre•tend•ed	<u>hidd</u>en	enough
<u>o</u>ver	t<u>i</u>mes	mo•ment	<u>strutt</u>ed	prey
A2 Rhyming Words	**B2** Schwa		<u>wing</u>ed	yourself
floor	<u>a</u>bove	body	<u>shout</u>ed	
door	<u>a</u>greed	during	<u>realiz</u>ed	
poor	<u>a</u>lone	pretended		
		moment		

4. MORPHOGRAPHS AND AFFIXES Have students read each underlined part, then the word.

Ⓐ	fin<u>al</u>	numer<u>al</u>	fiction<u>al</u>	nation<u>al</u>
Ⓑ	<u>dis</u>tance	mountain<u>ous</u>	tired<u>ly</u>	liv<u>able</u>

5. GENERALIZATION Have students read the paragraph silently, then out loud. (New words: barn, daytime, upside)

The forest animals were cleaning up the mountain. Everyone was helping but Bat. Bat spent his days hanging upside-down in the barn.

Eagle said, "Bat, you are lazy. Come work!"

Bat said, "I cannot work during the daytime. I must stay where it is dark."

Bear said, "Then you must work at night."

That is what Bat did. While the others slept, Bat worked. He worked all through the night, and everyone was happy.

BUILDING MASTERY (Reminder)

For each task, have students work first on accuracy and then on fluency. Have fun! Practice words multiple times in varied ways. Have students whisper the words, squeak the words, and read the sounds and words in a rhythm.

GENTLE CORRECTIONS

If you hear an error, write the word on the board.

Have all students identify the difficult sound and then blend the word.

Periodically, repeat practice of the difficult word.

GENERALIZATION (Reminder)

The generalization task provides an opportunity for you to informally assess students' ability to read new words that have not been pretaught.

CHAPTER 3 INSTRUCTIONS
Students read Chapter 3 with the teacher.

COMPREHENSION PROCESSES
Remember, Understand, Apply

PROCEDURES

1. Reviewing Chapter 2

Explaining—Action; Identifying—Who

• Have students turn to page 69. If time permits, have students reread Chapter 2 with you. Quickly discuss the questions from Chapter 2, Setting a Purpose. Say something like:
Yesterday, you read Chapter 2 on your own. Let's see what you found out.
What did Bat do during the second battle between the birds and the mammals? (He hid in the hollow tree.) Who won in Chapter 2? (The birds won.)
How did Bat try to trick the winners? (He showed the birds how he could fly, but he hid his teeth.)

2. Introducing Chapter 3

Identifying—Title; Predicting; Inferring—Lesson; Using Vocabulary—trickster
Discuss the title and main characters. Say something like:
What's the title of this chapter? (The End of the War) This chapter concludes the story. What do you think will happen to Bat in this chapter? (Bat will get into trouble.)
What lesson do you think Grandfather is trying to teach Gray Cloud? (You shouldn't pretend to be something you're not. You shouldn't be a trickster.)

3. First Reading
• Ask questions and discuss the story as indicated by the gray text.
• Mix group and individual turns, independent of your voice.
Have students work toward a group accuracy goal of 0–4 errors.
• After reading the story, practice any difficult words.
Reread the story if students have not reached the accuracy goal.

4. Second Reading, Timed Readings: Repeated Reading

• As time allows, have students do Timed Readings while others follow along.
• Time individuals for 30 seconds and encourage each child to work for a personal best.
• Determine words correct per minute. Record student scores.

5. Partner or Whisper Reading: Repeated Reading

Before beginning independent work, have students finger track and partner or whisper read.

6. Comprehension and Skill Work
For students on a 6-Day Plan, tell them they will do Comprehension and Skill Activities 3 and 4 after they read Chapter 3. Guide practice, as needed. For teacher directions, see pages 40 and 41. (For 8- to 11-Day Plans, see the Lesson Planner, page 9.)

7. Homework 2: Repeated Reading

WITH THE TEACHER

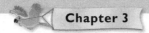 **Chapter 3**

The End of the War

Why do you think the war ends in this chapter?

The war went on. The mammals won four times, and the birds won four times. Finally, they all got tired of fighting. Bear and Eagle agreed to talk.

Eagle said, "Most of us Winged Ones live in the trees. We fly above the forest. We build our nests in the branches."

Bear said, "Most of us Four-Foots live on the floor of the forest. We sleep on the ground."

Eagle said, "There is room for all of us." All the animals agreed to share the forest. That night, there was a big party.

Bat strutted around, saying, "Oh boy, the war's over. Yippee! Let's eat!"

Why did the fighting stop?[1] What did the animals agree to do?[2] Why was there a big party?[3] What did Bat do?[4]

71

COMPREHENDING AS YOU GO

[1] **Understand:** Explaining (The birds and the mammals got tired of fighting.)

[2] **Remember:** Identifying—What (The animals agreed to share the forest.)

[3] **Apply:** Inferring (They had a big party because the war was over . . .)

[4] **Remember:** Identifying—What (Bat strutted around and said, "Oh, boy, the war's over. Yippee! Let's eat!")

72

36

THE WAR BETWEEN BIRDS AND MAMMALS

Bear said to Eagle, "Look, there is Bat. He is a Four-Footed One."

Eagle said, "No, Bat is a Winged One." At that moment, Bear and Eagle realized what Bat had done, so they made a new rule for Bat.

Bear and Eagle told Bat, "You hid in a hollow tree and pretended to be what you are not. From now on, you must always hide during the daytime. You must live in dark and hidden places. You can come out only at night. Only at night can you hunt for food for yourself and your family. You may not shout or speak. You cannot sing like birds or growl like other mammals."

So it is to this day. Bat hides in the daytime. He hangs upside down in caves, barns, and other hidden places. It is only at night that Bat comes out to hunt. When he does come out at night, Bat eats, and eats, and eats!

What did Eagle and Bear tell Bat?[1] Why does Bat hide in the daytime and come out only at night?[2] Do you think Bat is a mammal or a bird?[3]

73

COMPREHENDING
AS YOU GO

[1] **Remember:** Identifying—What (They told Bat that he has to hide during the day and come out only at night. They told him he couldn't shout or speak.)

[2] **Understand:** Explaining (Bat has to hide during the day because he tried to trick the others.)

[3] **Analyze:** Drawing Conclusions (Bat is a mammal because he has sharp teeth. Bat is a bird because he can fly.)

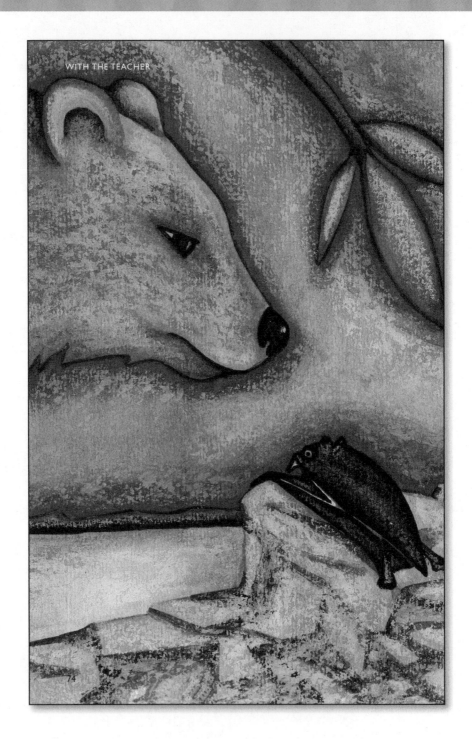

8. Introducing the Story Comparison Matrix

Using Graphic Organizer

Say something like:

Let's look at the story comparison chart. This matrix will help us see how the two legends are the same and how they are . . . (different).

Look at the first row. What two legends will we compare? (Centipede and . . .)

9. Comparing and Contrasting Story Elements

Identifying—Setting, Main Character, Problem, Action, Conclusion, Lesson; Comparing/Contrasting; Drawing Conclusions

Now look at the row for Setting. Where and when did "Centipede and Grandmother Spider" take place?

(in the mountain caves, when the world was new)

Where did "The War Between Birds and the Mammals" take place?

(in the forest, long, long ago)

According to legend, which story took place first?

(Centipede and Grandmother Spider)

How can you tell?

(During "The War Between Birds and Mammals," the birds and mammals were no longer living in the caves. They were living in the forest.)

Discuss how each of the remaining story elements are the same or different.

WITH THE TEACHER

Story Comparison

Legends

Legend	Centipede and Grandmother Spider	The War Between Birds and Mammals
Setting Where and when	In the mountain caves when the world was new	In the forest Long ago
Main Trickster Character	Centipede	Bat
Problem	Centipede did not have enough legs for his body.	The Birds and Mammals went to war with each other.
Action	Centipede took legs from the insects who slept.	While the animals fought, Bat hid. Then he pretended to be whichever type of animal had won.
Conclusion	Centipede must live under rocks. Insects will be prey for many animals.	Bat can only come out at night.
Lesson	Don't try to trick others.	Don't try to trick others. Be who you are.

75

VISUALIZING AND ILLUSTRATING

COMPREHENSION PROCESSES

Remember, Understand

WRITING TRAITS

Conventions—Period

Identifying—What
Visualizing, Illustrating

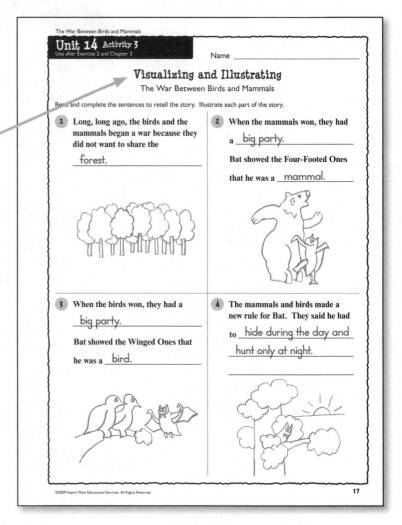

The War Between Birds and Mammals

Unit 14 Activity 3
Use after Exercise 2 and Chapter 3

Name _____

Visualizing and Illustrating
The War Between Birds and Mammals

Read and complete the sentences to retell the story. Illustrate each part of the story.

1 Long, long ago, the birds and the mammals began a war because they did not want to share the

forest.

2 When the mammals won, they had a _big party._

Bat showed the Four-Footed Ones that he was a _mammal._

3 When the birds won, they had a _big party._

Bat showed the Winged Ones that he was a _bird._

4 The mammals and birds made a new rule for Bat. They said he had to _hide during the day and hunt only at night._

©2009 Sopris West Educational Services. All Rights Reserved.   17

PROCEDURES

For each step, demonstrate and guide practice, as needed. Then have students complete the page independently.

Sentence Completion, Illustrating—Specific Instructions (Items 1–4)

• Have students read and complete each sentence. Tell students this activity retells the story.

You are going to complete the sentences to retell the story.

Read the sentence in the first box. (Long, long ago, the birds and the mammals began a war because they did not want to share the . . . *blank.*

What didn't they want to share? (the forest)

Yes, they were silly. There's plenty of room in a forest for the birds and mammals.

You'll write *forest* in the blank for number one.

Remind students to end each sentence with a period.

Repeat as needed for boxes 2, 3, and 4.

• Have students illustrate each sentence. Encourage them to visualize what they will draw in each box and to include as many details as possible. Say something like:

To illustrate the sentences in each box, you can first imagine, or visualize, what the sentences describe. Remember, visualizing helps you understand what you are reading. Read the first sentence with the correct word in the blank. (Long, long ago, the birds and the mammals began a war because they did not want to share the forest.)

Can you imagine what that would look like? (The birds are swooping down on the mammals. The mammals would leap at the birds.) How do you think the animals would look? (angry)

What else could be in the picture? (trees, shrubs . . .)

Yes, those details will make your illustrations just great! When you start drawing, you may want to look in your book for more ideas.

STORY COMPARISON

COMPREHENSION PROCESSES

Remember, Understand, Analyze

WRITING TRAITS

Conventions—Period

Using Graphic Organizer
Comparing/Contrasting
Identifying—Setting,
Explaining—Problem,
Conclusion, Lesson
Using Vocabulary—legend, trickster
Sentence Completion

The War Between Birds and Mammals

Unit 14 Activity 4
Use after Exercise 2 and Chapter 3

Name _____

Story Comparison

Complete the matrix below to compare the two legends you read. Circle whether the story element is the same or different.

Legend	Centipede and Grandmother Spider	The War Between Birds and Mammals	Same or Different
Setting Where and When	• in the mountains • when the world was new	• in the forest • long, long ago	same (different)
Main Trickster	Centipede	Bat	same (different)
Problem	Centipede didn't have enough legs.	The birds and the mammals went to war with each other.	same (different)
Action	While the insects slept, Centipede stole two legs from each insect and put them on himself.	While the animals were at war, Bat hid. When the mammals won, he pretended he was a mammal. When the birds won, he pretended he was a bird.	same (different)
Conclusion for the Trickster	Centipede was told to hide under leaves and rocks.	Bat was told to hide during the day and to hunt at night.	(same) (Both were punished.)
Lesson for the Trickster	Don't try to trick others.	Don't try to trick others.	(same) different

18

©2009 Sopris West Educational Services. All Rights Reserved.

PROCEDURES

For each step, demonstrate and guide practice, as needed. Then have students complete the page independently.

Compare/Contrast: Matrix—Specific Instructions

- Have students read the instructions. Say something like:

  Read the directions. (Complete the matrix below to compare the two legends you read. Circle whether the story element is the same or different.)

  Read the headings. The first column is about . . . (Centipede and Grandmother Spider).

  The second column is about . . . (The War Between Birds and Mammals).

- Orally guide students through the matrix only as needed. Say something like:

  Think back to the two legends we just finished reading. You're going to compare the two legends by figuring out how they are the same and different—just like we did in our storybooks.

  Look at the boxes. Touch the column that tells about "Centipede and Grandmother Spider."

  Touch the column that tells about "The War Between Birds and Mammals."

  The first row tells about the setting. Where and when did "Centipede and Grandmother Spider" take place? (in the mountains, when the world was new)

  Where and when did "The War Between Birds and Mammals" take place?

  (in the forest, long ago)

  Is the setting the same in both legends? (no)

  That's right. So, what word should you circle in the last column? (different)

- Have students complete the items independently.

41

❶ SOUND REVIEW
Use selected Sound Cards from Units 1–14.

❷ SHIFTY WORD BLENDING
For each word, have students say the underlined sound. Then have them sound out the word smoothly and say it. Use the words in sentences, as appropriate.

PACING
Exercise 3a should take about 10 minutes, allowing about 10 minutes for the Focus Lesson.

❸ ACCURACY AND FLUENCY BUILDING
- For each task, have students say any underlined part, then read the word.
- Set a pace. Then have students read the whole words in each task and column.
- Provide repeated practice, building accuracy first, then fluency.

B1. Word Endings
Have students read any underlined word, then the word with an ending.
Note: Tell students you drop the <u>e</u> when you add -*ly* to "true."

C1. Multisyllabic Words
- For the list of words divided by syllables, have students read each syllable, then the whole word. Use the word in a sentence, as appropriate.
- For the list of whole words, build accuracy and then fluency.

scorpion	Another member of the arachnid family is the . . . *scorpion.*
billowy	The boat's sail was . . . *billowy.*
anatomy	In biology class, we studied human . . . *anatomy.*
skeleton	All the bones in your body are called your . . . *skeleton.*
ordinary	Mike did everything he usually did. It was an . . . *ordinary* . . . day.
backbones	Mammals have . . . *backbones.*
classify	When scientists put animals in groups, they . . . *classify* . . . them.

D1. Tricky Words
- For each Tricky Word, have students use the sounds and word parts they know to silently sound out the word. Use the word in a sentence to help with pronunciation.
- If the word is unfamiliar, tell students the word.

young	A child who is two years old is very . . . *young.*
salmon	A fish that lives in the sea but swims up a river to lay eggs is a . . . *salmon.*
through	Alice in Wonderland went . . . *through* . . . the looking glass.
although	I will eat vanilla ice cream . . . *although* . . . I like chocolate better.
characteristics	Brown eyes and brown hair were two of the boy's . . . *characteristics.*

- Have students go back and read the whole words in the column.

❹ MORPHOGRAPHS AND AFFIXES
- Have students read the underlined part, then the word.
- Repeat practice with whole words, mixing group and individual turns. Build accuracy, then fluency.

❺ GENERALIZATION: READING NEW WORDS IN PARAGRAPHS
- Have students read the paragraph silently, then out loud. Tell students to use the sounds and word parts they know to read any difficult words.
- Repeat practice, as needed.

Incredible Flying Machine

Unit 14 Exercise 3a
Use before Chapter 1

1. SOUND REVIEW Use selected Sound Cards from Units 1–14.

2. SHIFTY WORD BLENDING For each word, have students say the underlined part, sound out smoothly, then read the word.

| b<u>e</u>nd | be<u>ck</u> | b<u>u</u>ck | <u>d</u>uck | dus<u>k</u> |

3. ACCURACY/FLUENCY BUILDING For each column, have students say any underlined part, then read each word. Next, have them read the column.

A1 Mixed Practice	B1 Word Endings	C1 Multisyllabic Words		D1 Tricky Words
wh<u>ir</u>l	<u>hatch</u>ed	scor•pi•on	scorpion	young
c<u>a</u>pe	<u>wrapp</u>ed	bil•low•y	billowy	salmon
flutt<u>er</u>	<u>elephant</u>s	a•nat•o•my	anatomy	through
gl<u>i</u>de	<u>relat</u>ed	skel•e•ton	skeleton	although
f<u>ea</u>thers		or•di•nar•y	ordinary	characteristics
b<u>ir</u>th	true	back•bones	backbones	
p<u>er</u>haps	truly	clas•si•fy	classify	
	baby			
	babies			

4. MORPHOGRAPHS AND AFFIXES Have students read the underlined word part, then the word.

| obv<u>ious</u> | obvious<u>ly</u> | <u>de</u>scribe | <u>dental</u> | <u>be</u>witching |

5. GENERALIZATION Have students read the paragraph silently, then out loud. (New words: pigeons, ostriches, catfish, trout)

Scientists put animals into groups. Eagles, robins, pigeons, and ostriches are birds. Ants, bees, and grasshoppers are insects. Spiders and scorpions are arachnids. People and dogs are mammals.

What do you think catfish, trout, and salmon are?

16

LEARNING FROM MISTAKES
(Reminder)

Mistakes are an important part of learning!

- If you hear a mistake, say something like: *Oops, that was hard, but we can get it!*
- Demonstrate or guide students on the correct skill or strategy (sound, sounding out, reading a word by parts . . .).
- Have the group practice the skill.
- Make sure the individual who made the mistake has an opportunity to demonstrate that he or she worked hard and got it.

Give descriptive feedback. *[Diego], you worked hard, and now you can read the tricky word* through.

CLASSIFYING

PURPOSE

FOCUS LESSON Skills and Strategies

The purpose of this lesson is to provide explicit instruction in how to use a classification chart that explains how animals are grouped. The lesson prepares students for Comprehension and Skill Work. Students do not write in their books but will watch and respond as you guide them through the lesson.

No Prep: For this Focus Lesson, students can follow along in their *Exercise Book*.

COMPREHENSION PROCESSES

Understand, Analyze

PROCEDURES

❶ INTRODUCTION

Explain the purpose of the lesson. Say something like:

Today, we're going to learn how to group animals by using a chart.

When we group things, we classify them.

Scientists spend a lot of time studying different animals to determine what group to put them in.

Today, you get to learn how to classify animals just like scientists do.

❷ CLASSIFYING ANIMALS

Using Graphic Organizer—Hierarchy Chart; Using Vocabulary—classify; Classifying

Guide responses and demonstrate how to write each response.

Everyone, look at the chart. Find number 1.

What's the first group on the chart? (birds)

Look at the animals under the bird group.

What animals are in the bird group? (emus and eagles)

There's also a question mark.

Look at the pictures under the heading "What's what?"

What's another animal that should go in the bird group? (ostriches)

Repeat with quail and parrots.

You just classified three more animals! What did you do? (We classified three animals.)

Now look at number 2. What's the second group on the chart? (mammals)

What animals are in the mammal group? (bears, elephants)

Look at the pictures under the heading "What's what?" again.

What's another animal that should go in the mammal group? (monkeys)

Repeat with zebras and rabbits.

What did you just do? (We classified three more animals.)

You are doing the job of a scientist called a taxonomist.

Taxonomists try to figure out what class, or group, to put different plants and animals in.

Next, we're going to learn the real story about bats and how to classify them!

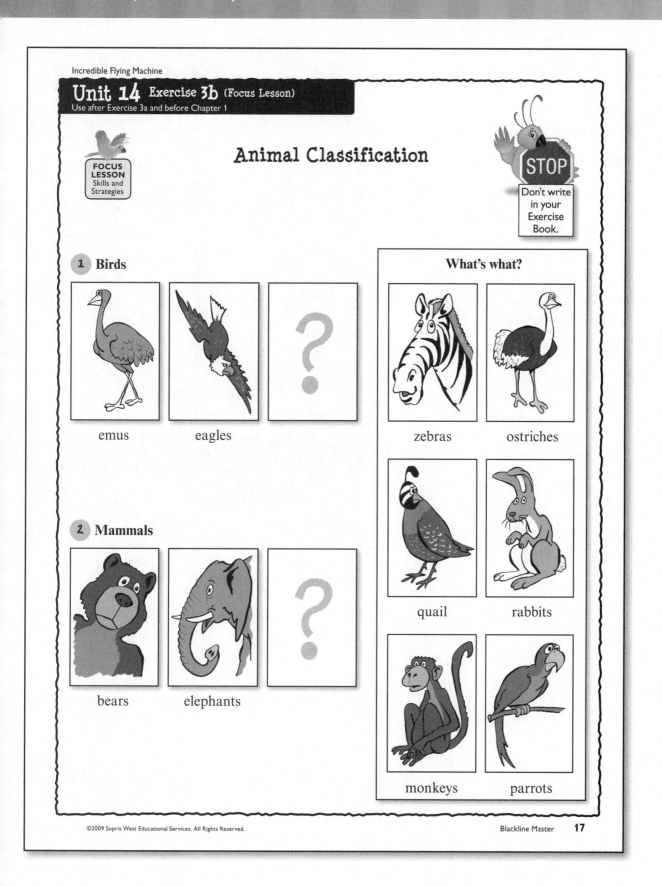

Incredible Flying Machine

Unit 14 Exercise 3b (Focus Lesson)
Use after Exercise 3a and before Chapter 1

FOCUS LESSON Skills and Strategies

Animal Classification

STOP
Don't write in your Exercise Book.

1 Birds

emus   eagles   ?

2 Mammals

bears   elephants   ?

What's what?

zebras   ostriches

quail   rabbits

monkeys   parrots

Blackline Master **17**

COMPREHENSION PROCESSES

Remember, Understand, Apply, Analyze

PROCEDURES

1. Introducing the Story

Identifying—Title; Viewing

Have students turn to page 76 in their storybook. Say something like:

What's the title of this story?
(Incredible Flying Machine)

Look at the picture. What do you see?
(hundreds of bats)

It must be an awesome sight to see hundreds of bats flying through the evening sky.

Incredible Flying Machine
by Marilyn Sprick

K-W-L
(modified)

Bats

What do we think we know?	What do we want to know?	What did we learn?

76

2. **Using K-W-L (modified)**

Using Graphic Organizer; Priming Background Knowledge; Generating Ideas; Asking Questions; Using Vocabulary—dangerous

- Use chart paper or three columns on a chalkboard to make a K-W-L chart.
- Remind students that reading nonfiction allows us to gain knowledge. Then have students identify what they think they know about bats. Say something like:

  What makes reading nonfiction fun? (We learn new facts. We get smarter.) That's right. You gain new knowledge, and that makes you smarter! Sometimes, new information even makes us change the way we think about something. Knowledge is always very powerful.

  We're going to do another K-W-L chart. First, we're going to identify what we think we know about bats. I think bats are related to mice, so I'm going to write that on the board.

  What do you *think* you know about bats? (Bats are dangerous. Bats bite people. Bats come out only at night.)

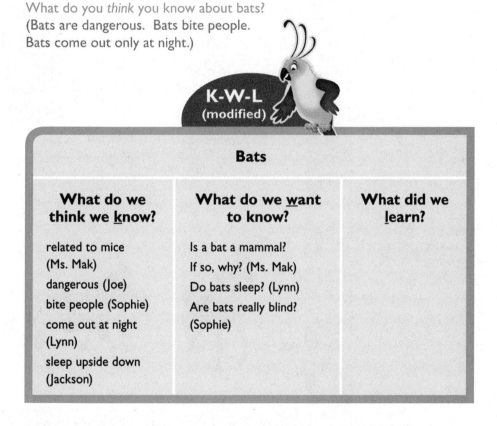

K-W-L (modified)

Bats

What do we think we <u>k</u>now?	What do we <u>w</u>ant to know?	What did we <u>l</u>earn?
related to mice (Ms. Mak)	Is a bat a mammal?	
dangerous (Joe)	If so, why? (Ms. Mak)	
bite people (Sophie)	Do bats sleep? (Lynn)	
come out at night (Lynn)	Are bats really blind? (Sophie)	
sleep upside down (Jackson)		

- Think aloud as you demonstrate how to ask questions. Then have students generate questions about bats. Say something like:

  I really do think bats are mammals. So I have two questions that I would like answered. Is a bat a mammal? If so, why? What questions do you have? (Do bats sleep? Are bats really blind . . .)

  Those are all great questions. This should be an interesting selection! We will all be bat experts.

COMPREHENSION PROCESSES

Understand, Apply, Analyze

PROCEDURES

1. Introducing Vocabulary

> ☆ obvious ☆ obviously
> ☆ characteristics ☆ classify
> ☆ mammal

- For each vocabulary word, have students read the word by parts, then read the whole word.
- Read the student-friendly explanations to students as they follow with their fingers. Then have students use the vocabulary word by following the gray text.
- Review and discuss the photos.

USING VOCABULARY

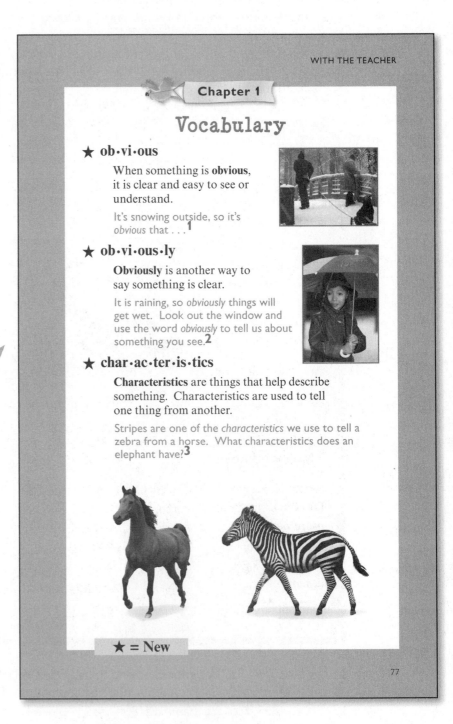

WITH THE TEACHER

Chapter 1

Vocabulary

★ **ob·vi·ous**

When something is **obvious**, it is clear and easy to see or understand.

It's snowing outside, so it's *obvious* that . . .[1]

★ **ob·vi·ous·ly**

Obviously is another way to say something is clear.

It is raining, so *obviously* things will get wet. Look out the window and use the word *obviously* to tell us about something you see.[2]

★ **char·ac·ter·is·tics**

Characteristics are things that help describe something. Characteristics are used to tell one thing from another.

Stripes are one of the *characteristics* we use to tell a zebra from a horse. What characteristics does an elephant have?[3]

★ = New

77

❶ **Apply:** Using Vocabulary—obvious (it's cold)

❷ **Apply:** Using Vocabulary—obviously (It's sunny today, so obviously, we won't need our umbrellas.)

❸ **Apply:** Using Vocabulary—characteristics (Elephants are large mammals. They have big ears, a long trunk . . .)

2. Now You Try It!
- Read or paraphrase the directions.
- Have students read the word by parts, then read the whole word.
- Have students explain or define the word in their own words.
- Have students turn to the appropriate page in the glossary and discuss how their definition is the same as or different from the glossary's. Your students may like their definition better.

Note: By defining a word in their own words, students are demonstrating depth of word knowledge. Verbatim responses only demonstrate memorization. Encourage paraphrasing.

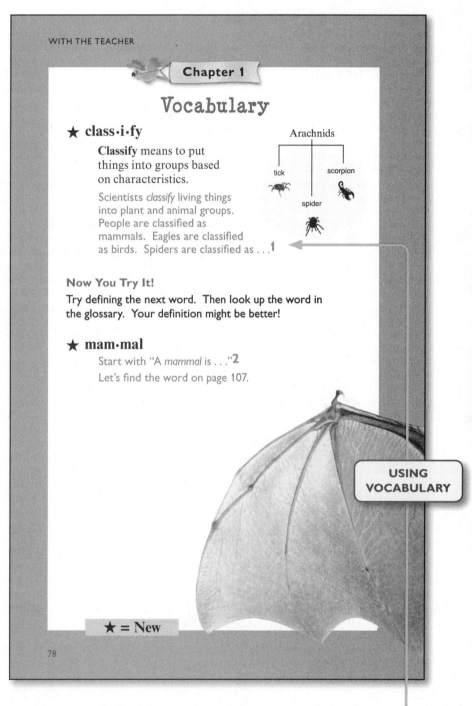

WITH THE TEACHER

Chapter 1

Vocabulary

★ **class·i·fy**

Classify means to put things into groups based on characteristics.

Scientists *classify* living things into plant and animal groups. People are classified as mammals. Eagles are classified as birds. Spiders are classified as . . .**1**

Arachnids

tick   scorpion

spider

Now You Try It!
Try defining the next word. Then look up the word in the glossary. Your definition might be better!

★ **mam·mal**

Start with "A *mammal* is . . ."**2**
Let's find the word on page 107.

USING VOCABULARY

★ = New

78

❶ Analyze: Classifying; **Understand:** Using Vocabulary—classify, arachnids (arachnids)

❷ Understand: Defining and Using Vocabulary—mammal; Using Glossary (A mammal is an animal that has a backbone and hair or fur. Mammals breathe air, give birth to their babies, and take care of their young.)

CHAPTER 1 INSTRUCTIONS
Students read Chapter 1 with the teacher.

COMPREHENSION PROCESSES
Understand, Apply, Analyze

PROCEDURES

1. Introducing Chapter 1
   - Read the poem on page 79 with students.
   - Have students read the chapter title on page 80.
   - Ask the gray text questions under the chapter title.

2. First Reading
   - Ask questions and discuss the story as indicated by the gray text.
   - Mix group and individual turns, independent of your voice.
     Have students work toward a group accuracy goal of 0–3 errors.
     Quietly keep track of errors made by all students in the group.
   - After reading the story, practice any difficult words.
     Reread the story if students have not reached the accuracy goal.

3. Second Reading, Short Passage Practice: Developing Prosody
   - Demonstrate expressive, fluent reading of the first two paragraphs.
   - Guide practice with your voice.
   - Provide individual turns while others track with their fingers and whisper read.
   - Repeat with one paragraph at a time.

4. Partner or Whisper Reading: Repeated Reading
Before beginning independent work, have students finger track and partner or whisper read.

5. Comprehension and Skill Work
Tell students they will do a Comprehension and Skill Classification Chart after they read Chapter 1. Guide practice, as needed. For teacher directions, see pages 57–59.

6. Homework 3: Repeated Reading

> **CORRECTING DECODING ERRORS**
> During story reading, gently correct any error, then have students reread the sentence.

INCREDIBLE FLYING MACHINE

Billowy bat, did you call?
Are you a bird after all?

With cape-like wings,
You whirl and flutter.
Your hand-like wings bend and flex.

Bewitching bat in the air,
Are you a bird after all?

79

FOCUS ON VIEWING

Inferring

Have students look carefully at the bat. Say something like:

The poem said the bat has hand-like wings. Why do you think the author used the words *hand-like wings*? (It looks like it has fingers holding up its wings.)

Now that you've had a chance to look at a bat up close, let's think about the question the poem asks the bat. "Are you a bird after all?" Raise your hand if you think a bat is a bird. Raise your hand if you think a bat is a mammal.

WITH THE TEACHER

Chapter 1

Bird or Mammal?

Look at the chart. What do you think you'll learn in this chapter?[1]

All over the world, millions and millions of bats take flight at dusk. What are these flying creatures of the night?

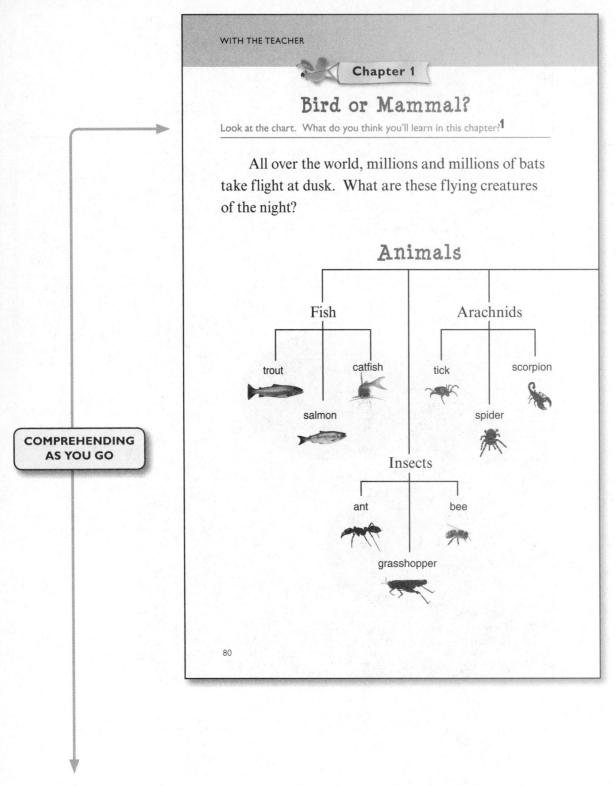

Animals

Fish   Arachnids

trout   catfish   tick   scorpion

salmon   spider

Insects

ant   bee

grasshopper

80

COMPREHENDING AS YOU GO

❶ Apply: Viewing; Inferring; Using Graphic Organizer—Hierarchy Chart (We will learn about different types of animals. We'll learn whether a bat is a bird or a mammal.)

INCREDIBLE FLYING MACHINE

Scientists classify living things based on how they look, their anatomy, and how they are related to other animals.

Ants and grasshoppers are insects. Spiders and scorpions are arachnids. Eagles and ostriches are birds. People and elephants are mammals. But what is a bat?

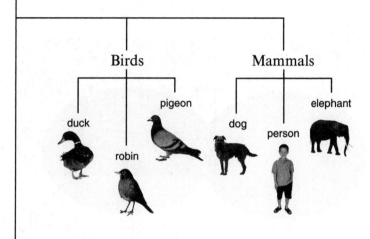

Birds

Mammals

duck

pigeon

robin

dog

person

elephant

What kinds, or groups, of animals are on the chart?¹Find the arachnids. Name three arachnids.²Find the group people are in. What are people?³ What do you think a bat is?⁴

81

COMPREHENDING AS YOU GO

➊ **Understand:** Viewing; Using Graphic Organizer—Hierarchy Chart; Explaining (The chart shows fish, insects, arachnids, birds, and mammals.)

➋ **Understand:** Locating Information; **Analyze:** Classifying (A tick, a scorpion, and a spider are all arachnids.)

➌ **Understand:** Locating Information; Using Vocabulary—mammal; **Analyze:** Classifying (People are mammals.)

➍ **Analyze:** Inferring; **Understand:** Using Vocabulary—mammal (A bat is a mammal. A bat is a bird.)

WITH THE TEACHER

Obviously, bats are not fish, insects, or arachnids. Perhaps they are birds. Like most birds, bats fly. Like all birds, bats have wings and backbones. Yet, as the legend tells us, bats are not birds. They don't lay eggs, and they don't have feathers.

Are bats mammals? Mammals have backbones, and they have fur or hair. They give birth to their babies and take care of their young.

Look at this bat skeleton. Does it have a backbone?

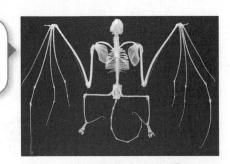

Now look at this bat. Does it have hair or fur?

What *characteristics* do *mammals* have?**1** Do bats have backbones?**2** Do bats have fur?**3**

82

COMPREHENDING
AS YOU GO

❶ **Understand:** Explaining; Using Vocabulary—characteristics, mammal (Mammals have backbones and fur or hair. They give birth to their babies and take care of their young.)

❷ **Analyze:** Viewing, Inferring (Yes, bats have backbones.)

❸ **Analyze:** Viewing, Inferring (Yes, bats have fur.)

INCREDIBLE FLYING MACHINE

Look at the baby bat. This baby bat was born live. It was not hatched from an egg. The baby bat drinks its mother's milk. The baby is wrapped in its mother's wing where it is warm and safe. When the baby bat is older, its mother will teach it how to fly and find food.

Do bats give birth to their babies and take care of their young?[1]

83

COMPREHENDING AS YOU GO

❶ **Apply:** Inferring (Yes, bats give birth to their babies and take care of their young.)

WITH THE TEACHER

With all of these characteristics, scientists classify bats as mammals, but they are not ordinary mammals. Although some mammals glide through the air, bats are the only mammals that can truly fly.

Think and Talk

CLASSIFICATION

1. Why are bats classified as mammals?

INFERENCE

2. What makes a bat an extraordinary mammal?

INFERENCE

3. Why do some people think bats are birds?

84

❶ **Analyze:** Classifying; **Apply:** Explaining; Using Vocabulary—classify, mammal (Bats are classified as mammals because they have backbones and fur. Like all mammals, they also give birth to their babies, and they take care of their young.)

❷ **Apply:** Inferring, Explaining; **Understand:** Using Vocabulary—mammal (Bats are the only mammals that can fly.)

❸ **Apply:** Inferring, Explaining (Some people think bats are birds because they can fly.)

CLASSIFICATION CHART

COMPREHENSION PROCESSES

Apply, Analyze

Using Graphic Organizer; Classifying

SPECIAL NOTE
Your students will complete a classification chart and fact summary. For ease of use, pull pages 19–22 out of *Activity Book 3* and staple them together.

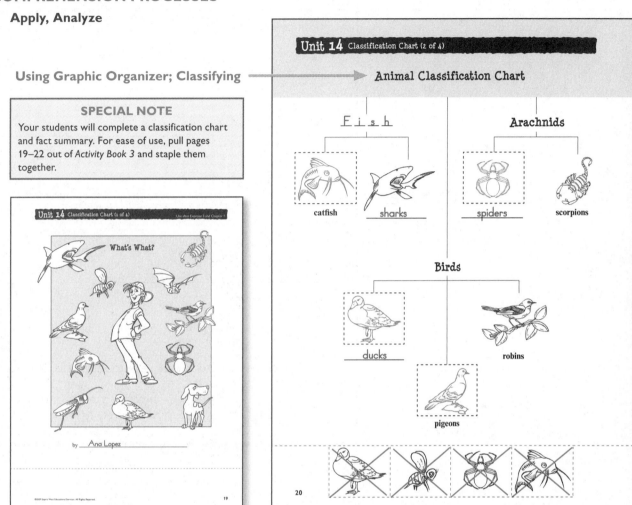

PROCEDURES

For each step, demonstrate and guide practice, as needed. Then have students complete the pages independently.

1. Preparation

After pages 19–22 have been removed from *Activity Book 3*, have students write their names on the cover. Next, have students carefully cut off the bottom strip and cut out the pictures.

2. Classification: Hierarchy Chart—Specific Instructions
- Have students classify and glue the pictures into the correct group or class.
- Have students complete the chart by filling in the missing labels.

CLASSIFICATION CHART

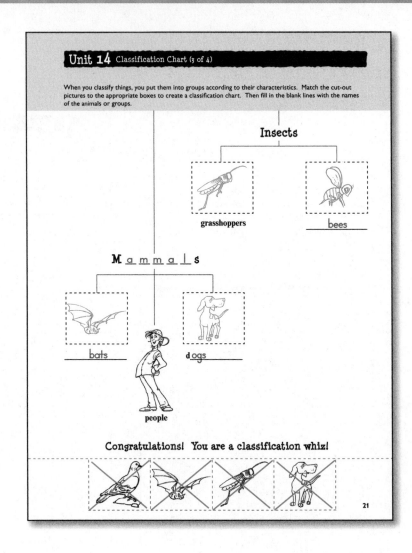

Unit 14 Classification Chart (3 of 4)

When you classify things, you put them into groups according to their characteristics. Match the cut-out pictures to the appropriate boxes to create a classification chart. Then fill in the blank lines with the names of the animals or groups.

Insects

grasshoppers   bees

M a m m a l s

bats   d ogs

people

Congratulations! You are a classification whiz!

21

FACT SUMMARY

COMPREHENSION PROCESSES

Remember, Apply

WRITING TRAITS

Conventions—Period

Using Graphic Organizer; Identifying—
Topic/Main Idea, Supporting Details
Sentence Completion

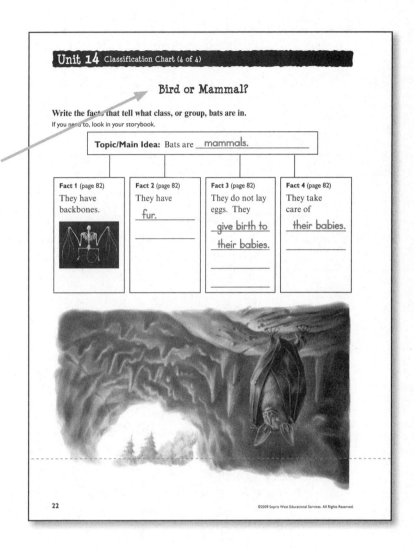

Unit 14 Classification Chart (4 of 4)

Bird or Mammal?

Write the facts that tell what class, or group, bats are in.
If you need to, look in your storybook.

Topic/Main Idea: Bats are ___mammals.___

Fact 1 (page 82)
They have backbones.

Fact 2 (page 82)
They have ___fur.___

Fact 3 (page 82)
They do not lay eggs. They ___give birth to their babies.___

Fact 4 (page 82)
They take care of ___their babies.___

22   ©2009 Sopris West Educational Services. All Rights Reserved.

PROCEDURES

For each step, demonstrate and guide practice, as needed. Then have students complete the page independently.

1. **Topic/Main Idea: Hierarchy Chart—Basic Instructions**
   Have students complete the Topic/Main Idea statement.

2. **Supporting Details: Hierarchy Chart—Specific Instructions**
   • Have students complete each fact that supports the main idea. Remind them to use a period.
   • Remind students that they can look back in their storybook to locate information.

❶ SOUND REVIEW

Use selected Sound Cards from Units 1–14.

❷ SOUND PRACTICE

- For each task, have students spell and say the focus sound in the gray bar. Next, have students read each underlined sound, the word, then the whole column.
- Repeat with each column, building accuracy first, then fluency.

❸ ACCURACY AND FLUENCY BUILDING

B1. Compound Words

Have students tell you what a compound word is. Then have students read the words.

A compound word is made of two . . . (small words). Yes, a compound word is made of two small words. Read the compound words.

C1. Multisyllabic Words

- For the list of words divided by syllables, have students read each syllable, then the whole word. Use the word in a sentence, as appropriate.
- For the list of whole words, build accuracy, then fluency.

fabric	Another word for cloth is . . . *fabric.*
pollen	The yellow powder a bee gets from flowers is called . . . *pollen.*
impressive	The acrobat's triple back flip was . . . *impressive.*
vampire	Monique had nightmares after watching a scary movie about a . . . *vampire.*
whistle	Put your lips together and blow air out to . . . *whistle.*
superb	Wow, that picture you drew was really, really great. It was . . . *superb.*
predators	Animals that hunt other animals for food are . . . *predators.*
carnivores	Animals that eat mostly meat are called . . . *carnivores.*
herbivores	Animals that eat only plants are called . . . *herbivores.*

E1. Tricky Words

- For each Tricky Word, have students use the sounds and word parts they know to silently sound out the word. Use the word in a sentence to help with pronunciation.
- If the word is unfamiliar, tell students the word.

machines	We went to the laundromat and saw lots of washing . . . *machines.*
weighs	The vet puts my dog on the scale to see how much he . . . *weighs.*
fruit	Apples are a kind of . . . *fruit.*
die	Little Jimmy was afraid his sick turtle would . . . *die.*
unusual	Something that is odd or that doesn't happen often is . . . *unusual.*
breaking	When I stepped on the glass, I could hear it . . . *breaking.*

- Have students go back and read the whole words in the column.

❹ PLACES

Tell students these are the names of places from the story. Have students use the sounds and word parts they know to figure out the words. Assist, as needed.

❺ MORPHOGRAPHS AND AFFIXES

★Have students practice reading *-ible* and the related words. Use each word in a sentence.

- For Row B, have students read the underlined part, then the word.

⑥ GENERALIZATION: READING NEW WORDS IN PARAGRAPHS
- Have students read the paragraph silently, then out loud. Tell students to use the sounds and word parts they know to read any difficult words.
- Repeat practice, as needed.

Incredible Flying Machine

Unit 14 Exercise 4
Use before Chapters 2 and 3

1. **SOUND REVIEW** Use selected Sound Cards from Units 1–14.

2. **SOUND PRACTICE** In each column, have students spell and say the sound, next say any underlined sound and the word, then read the column.

ee, ea	ou as in cloud	ce, ci	Rhyming Words
bl<u>ee</u>d	p<u>ou</u>nds	gra<u>ce</u>	tomatoes
t<u>ea</u>k	sn<u>ou</u>t	surfa<u>ce</u>	potatoes
rep<u>ea</u>ts	b<u>ou</u>nces	fas<u>ci</u>nated	mosquitoes

3. **ACCURACY/FLUENCY BUILDING** For each column, have students say any underlined part, then read each word. Next, have them read the column.

A1 Mixed Practice	B1 Compound Words	C1 Multisyllabic Words		D1 Tricky Words
sk<u>u</u>ll	wingspan	fa•bric	fabric	machines
all<u>ow</u>	teaspoons	pol•len	pollen	weighs
penn<u>y</u>	bumblebee	im•press•ive	impressive	fruit
upp<u>er</u>	tailbone	vam•pire	vampire	die
scar<u>y</u>	**B2 Related Words**	whis•*t*le	whistle	unusual
re<u>gi</u>ons	locate	su•perb	superb	breaking
	location	pred•a•tors	predators	
	echolocation	car•ni•vores	carnivores	
		her•bi•vores	herbivores	

4. **PLACES** Have students use the sounds and word parts they know to figure out the words.

Texas	Thailand	Southeast Asia	Central America

5. **MORPHOGRAPHS AND AFFIXES** Have students practice reading "-ible" and the related words. For Row B, have students read the underlined part, then the word.

Ⓐ	★-ible	flex<u>ible</u>	poss<u>ible</u>	incred<u>ible</u>	invis<u>ible</u>
Ⓑ	spind<u>ly</u>	direc<u>tion</u>	<u>un</u>knowing	success<u>ful</u>	

6. **GENERALIZATION** Have students read the paragraph silently, then out loud. (New words: compared, pandas, polar, endangered)

Ann's class is studying bears. Yesterday the class compared giant pandas and polar bears. They learned that giant pandas live in rain forests and polar bears live in cold Arctic regions. Polar bears are not endangered yet, but panda bears are. Both types of bears have lost habitat and could become extinct some day.

COMPREHENSION PROCESSES

Remember, Understand, Apply

PROCEDURES

Introducing Vocabulary

> ⭐flexible ⭐billow, locate
> ⭐location ⭐prey ⭐echo,
> predator ⭐endangered
> ⭐pollen

- For each vocabulary word, have students read the word by parts, then read the whole word.
- Read the student-friendly explanations to students as they follow with their fingers. Then have students use the vocabulary word by following the gray text.
- Review and discuss the photos and illustrations.

USING VOCABULARY

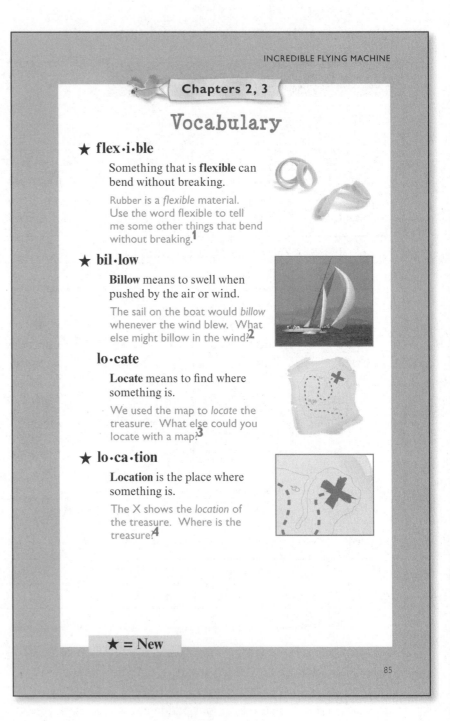

INCREDIBLE FLYING MACHINE

Chapters 2, 3

Vocabulary

★ **flex·i·ble**

Something that is **flexible** can bend without breaking.

Rubber is a *flexible* material. Use the word flexible to tell me some other things that bend without breaking.**1**

★ **bil·low**

Billow means to swell when pushed by the air or wind.

The sail on the boat would *billow* whenever the wind blew. What else might billow in the wind?**2**

lo·cate

Locate means to find where something is.

We used the map to *locate* the treasure. What else could you locate with a map?**3**

★ **lo·ca·tion**

Location is the place where something is.

The X shows the *location* of the treasure. Where is the treasure?**4**

★ = New

85

---

1 **Apply:** Using Vocabulary—flexible (Clay is flexible. Plastic straws are flexible . . .)

2 **Apply:** Using Vocabulary—billow (Sheets billow in the wind. Kites billow in the wind . . .)

3 **Apply:** Using Vocabulary—locate (I could locate my school, my state, and my country with a map.)

4 **Apply:** Using Vocabulary—location, treasure (The location of the treasure is at the X.)

WITH THE TEACHER

★ **prey**

Prey is an animal that is hunted and eaten by another animal.

A spider traps its *prey* in a web. What do spiders trap in their webs?**1**

★ **ech·o**

An **echo** is a sound that repeats because it bounces off a surface in its path.

I could hear the *echo* of my footsteps in the empty hallway. Where else have you heard an echo?**2**

pre·da·tor

A **predator** is an animal that hunts other animals for food.

A bat is a *predator* that hunts for insects. Why is a bat a predator?**3**

★ **en·dan·gered**

An animal or plant is **endangered** when it might become extinct.

There are not very many panda bears left. They are *endangered*. Can you name any other endangered animals?**4**

★ **pol·len**

Pollen is a yellow powder made by plants. Pollen helps plants grow seeds.

What do flowers make that helps them grow seeds?**5**

★ = New

86

USING VOCABULARY

❶ **Remember:** Using Vocabulary—prey (Spiders trap prey in their webs.)

❷ **Apply:** Making Connections; **Understand:** Using Vocabulary—echo (I heard an echo in a tunnel. I heard an echo at the top of a mountain. I could hear an echo in a cave . . .)

❸ **Understand:** Defining and Vocabulary—predator (A bat is a predator because it hunts insects for food.)

❹ **Apply:** Using Vocabulary—endangered (Blue whales are endangered animals. Green sea turtles are endangered.)

❺ **Understand:** Using Vocabulary—pollen (Flowers make pollen.)

CHAPTER 2 INSTRUCTIONS

Students read Chapter 2 with the teacher and Chapter 3 on their own.
Note: If you're working on an 8- to 11-Day Plan, you will read Chapter 3 with students.

COMPREHENSION PROCESSES

Remember, Understand, Apply, Analyze, Evaluate, Create

PROCEDURES

1. Reviewing Chapter 1

Classifying; Summarizing—Facts; Using Vocabulary—characteristics, mammal; Inferring

Have students turn to page 80. Quickly review some of the facts learned in Chapter 1. Say something like:

Let's see what we remember from yesterday.

Are bats birds or mammals? (Bats are mammals.)

What characteristics do mammals have? (They have backbones and fur, they give birth to babies, and they take care of their babies.)

Why is the bat an unusual or extraordinary mammal? (It can fly.)

2. Introducing Chapter 2 and Setting the Purpose

Identifying—Title

• Have students read the chapter title and answer the gray text question.

• Tell students they will learn things in this chapter that many people could not explain. Say something like:

When you finish this chapter, you will be very proud of yourself. You will be able to explain things that most people do not know.

3. First Reading

• Ask questions and discuss the story as indicated by the gray text.

• Mix group and individual turns, independent of your voice.
Have students work toward a group accuracy goal of 0–4 errors.
Quietly keep track of errors made by all students in the group.

• After reading the story, practice any difficult words.
Reread the story if students have not reached the accuracy goal.

4. Second Reading, Timed Readings: Repeated Reading

• As time allows, have students do Timed Readings while others follow along.

• Time individuals for 30 seconds and encourage each child to work for a personal best.

• Determine words correct per minute. Record student scores.

INCREDIBLE FLYING MACHINE

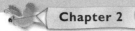

Chapter 2

Flying Machine

What do you think you'll learn about bats in this chapter?[1]

Bat Anatomy

A bat has a hard bony skeleton like yours. It has a skull, neck bone, backbone, two legs, and a tailbone.

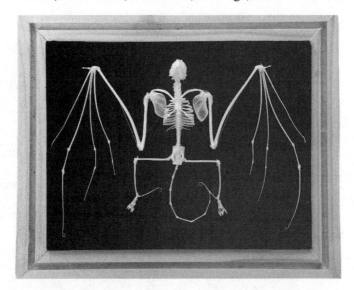

The bat's two upper arm bones are used to flap its wings. Bats have a small thumb and four long spindly fingers on each hand. The fingers stretch out and support the wing for flight.

Touch the bat's skull, the neck bone, backbone, legs, and tailbone.[2] What does a bat use its arm bones for?[3] How many fingers does a bat have on each hand?[4] How is a bat's skeleton the same as ours? How is it different?[5]

87

COMPREHENDING AS YOU GO

❶ **Apply:** Inferring (We will learn how bats fly. We'll learn how they are flying machines.)

❷ **Apply:** Demonstrating

❸ **Understand:** Explaining (The bat uses its arm bones to flap its wings.)

❹ **Understand:** Identifying (A bat has five fingers.)

❺ **Analyze:** Comparing/Contrasting (People and bats have skulls, neck bones, backbones, two legs, a tailbone, two arms, and hands with five fingers. Bats have longer tail bones and long spindly fingers.)

WITH THE TEACHER

A bat's wing is like a sail. Scientists call it a hand-wing. Thin, flexible skin stretches between the long fingers. The wings billow and change shape. These hand-wings allow bats to dart through the air and change direction quickly—like no other animal can. Scientists think bats are incredible. They are studying bats so that some day they can make bat-like flying machines.

 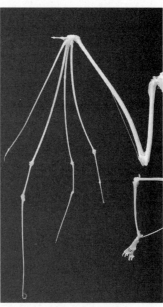

Just as the fabric of an umbrella stretches between the spokes, the thin skin of a bat's wing stretches between its fingers.

Describe a bat's wings.**1** Why are bats able to quickly change directions when flying?**2**

88

COMPREHENDING AS YOU GO

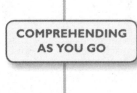

❶ **Understand:** Describing; Using Vocabulary—flexible (A bat's wing is like a sail. The wings are very thin and flexible. The wings stretch between the bat's fingers.)

❷ **Understand:** Explaining; Using Vocabulary—billow (A bat has hand-wings that billow and change shape. The long thin fingers can move very quickly.)

INCREDIBLE FLYING MACHINE

Bat Senses

Many bats hunt for insects at night. Small insects are hard to see in the dark, so many bats use sound to locate their prey. Sounds are made when waves of air move. Bats catch sound waves with their big ears.

Bats also use what is called echolocation. Instead of waiting for insects to make sounds, bats make sounds. They whistle, click, and snort through their noses. The sounds they make bounce back to them. Based on that echo, a bat knows how far away an insect is, whether it is to the right or left, and even how big it is. Wow! That's echolocation.

Touch the bat's big ears. Why do you think this bat has such big ears?**1**
Say echolocation. Explain what happens when a bat makes a noise.**2**What is this called?**3**

89

> **PRIMING BACKGROUND KNOWLEDGE**
>
> Before reading the page, say something like:
> In this section, you're going to learn about bat senses. They have a very special way to hear. They use echoes.
>
> If you were in a cave and hollered, "helloo," your voice would bounce off the cave walls and come back to you. Pretend you are my echo. Hellooo. (helloooooooo)
>
> When you finish the page, you'll be able to explain how bats use echoes in a very special way. You will be very smart!

COMPREHENDING AS YOU GO

1 **Apply:** Inferring, Explaining (Bats catch sound waves. The bat has big ears so it can catch sound waves.)

2 **Understand:** Explaining; Using Vocabulary—echo (When a bat makes noise, the sounds bounce off things around it. The bat uses the echo to tell where those things are.)

3 **Remember:** Identifying—What (This is called echolocation.)

WITH THE TEACHER

Many people think that bats can't see, but this is bat fiction. Bats see well. They use sight, hearing, and echolocation to hunt. Are bats successful predators? Judge for yourself. A colony of bats in Texas eats 500,000 pounds of mosquitoes in just one night. Wow again!

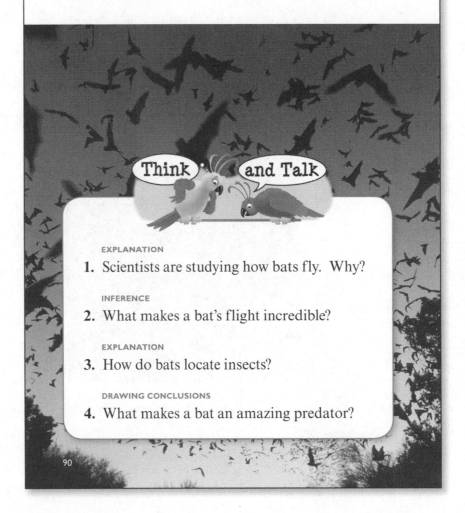

Think and Talk

EXPLANATION
1. Scientists are studying how bats fly. Why?

INFERENCE
2. What makes a bat's flight incredible?

EXPLANATION
3. How do bats locate insects?

DRAWING CONCLUSIONS
4. What makes a bat an amazing predator?

90

❶ **Understand:** Explaining; **Apply:** Inferring (Scientists are studying bats so that some day they can make bat-like flying machines. Bats are such great flyers that they think a bat-like flying machine would be better than an airplane or helicopter.)

❷ **Apply:** Inferring, Explaining; **Understand:** Using Vocabulary—mammal, allow (No other mammal can fly. A bat has special hand-wings that allow it to turn very quickly.)

❸ **Apply:** Explaining; **Understand:** Using Vocabulary—locate (Bats make sounds. Their echoes bounce off the insects back to the bat. The bat can locate the insect by using its echo.)

❹ **Analyze:** Drawing Conclusions; **Apply:** Explaining; Using Vocabulary—amazing, predator, locate, prey (Bats are amazing predators because they use sound waves to locate their prey—in the dark.)

CHAPTER 3 INSTRUCTIONS

Students read without the teacher, independently or with partners.
Note: If you're working on an 8- to 11-Day Plan, you will read Chapter 3 with students.

COMPREHENSION PROCESSES

Remember, Understand, Apply, Analyze, Create

PROCEDURES FOR READING ON YOUR OWN

1. Getting Ready

Have students turn to Chapter 3 on page 91.

2. Setting a Purpose

Explaining—Facts

Before students begin reading, say something like:

As you read the next pages, try to answer these questions:

- Where do bats live?
- What's the smallest bat?
- What's the largest bat?
- How does a vampire bat eat?

> **PREP NOTE**
> **Setting a Purpose**
> Write questions on a chalkboard, white board, or large piece of paper before working with your small group.

3. Reading on Your Own: Partner or Whisper Reading

- Have students take turns reading every other page with a partner or have students whisper read on their own.
- Continue having students track each word with their fingers.
- Have students ask themselves or their partners the gray text questions.

4. Comprehension and Skill Work

For students on a 6-Day Plan, tell them they will do Comprehension and Skill Activities 5 and 6 after they read Chapter 3 on their own. Guide practice, as needed. For teacher directions, see pages 75 and 76. (For 8- to 11-Day Plans, see the Lesson Planner, page 9.)

5. Homework 4: Repeated Reading

INCREDIBLE FLYING MACHINE

Chapter 3

Types of Bats

What do you already know about different types of bats?[1] What would you like to learn about different types of bats?[2]

Bats live all over the world, except in the polar regions where it is too cold. Bats live in forests and deserts, in cities, and in the country. They stay in caves, trees, under logs, and even in people's attics.

There are many different types of bats—about 1,100 in all. That's an impressive number! There are just 41 types of cats in the world and only three types of elephants.

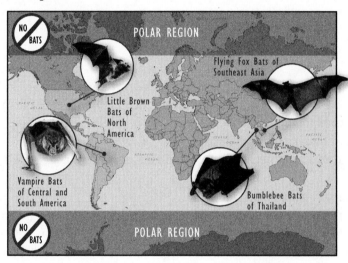

Name two facts that make bats interesting.[3]

91

COMPREHENDING AS YOU GO

❶ **Apply:** Priming Background Knowledge (Some bats are really small, and some are big . . .)

❷ **Create:** Generating Ideas, Asking Questions (How many kinds of bats are there? What kind of bats live in a cave? Do vampire bats really suck your blood?)

❸ **Understand:** Summarizing—Facts (Bats live all over the world. There are only 41 types of cats, but there are 1,100 types of bats . . .)

ON YOUR OWN

The Smallest Bat

The smallest bat is the bumblebee bat. It is also the smallest mammal in the world. This tiny bat weighs less than a penny. From tip to tip, its wings are six inches wide—about as wide as you can spread your hand.

Bumblebee bat

The bumblebee bat has big ears and a pig-like snout. Bumblebee bats live in Thailand. At dusk, these creatures fly around the tops of bamboo and teak trees, eating spiders and small insects. The bumblebee bat is a carnivore. Because of a loss of habitat, bumblebee bats are one of the most endangered animals on the planet. Some people think that there may be only about 130 bumblebee bats left in the world.

Describe the bumblebee bat.**1** Why is it *endangered?***2** Do you think bumblebee bats will be extinct by the time you are an adult? Why or why not?**3**

92

COMPREHENDING
AS YOU GO

❶ **Understand:** Describing; Using Vocabulary—carnivore (The bumblebee bat is very small. It has big ears and a pig-like snout. It is a carnivore . . .)

❷ **Understand:** Explaining; Using Vocabulary—endangered, habitat (The bumblebee bat is endangered because it has lost its habitat.)

❸ **Analyze:** Drawing Conclusions; **Apply:** Using Vocabulary—habitat, extinct (Yes, I think people will help the bumblebee bat get its habitat back. No, there aren't very many bumblebee bats left, so they will be *extinct* by the time I grow up . . .)

INCREDIBLE FLYING MACHINE

The Largest Bat

   The largest bat is Southeast Asia's flying fox. Compared to the bumblebee bat, the flying fox is huge. It weighs more than three pounds and has a wingspan five to six feet wide! That's almost as long as a bed. Flying foxes feed on fruit and pollen. These big bats are not very graceful herbivores. They often crash into their food!

Flying fox

How is the flying fox different from a bumblebee bat?[1]

93

COMPREHENDING AS YOU GO

❶ Analyze: Contrasting; **Apply:** Using Vocabulary—herbivore, carnivore (The flying fox is very large and has a wingspan of six feet. The bumblebee bat is very small and has a wingspan of six inches. The flying fox is an herbivore. The bumblebee bat is a carnivore.)

ON YOUR OWN

Vampire Bats

People are fascinated by vampire bats. These unusual animals are found only in South America and Central America. They drink the blood of cows, pigs, horses, and birds. Vampire bats fly close to the ground. They use sight, smell, and echolocation to locate sleeping animals. Then they make a small cut with their sharp teeth. When the animal begins to bleed, the bat laps up the blood while the unknowing animal sleeps. Each night, a vampire bat drinks about eight teaspoons of blood.

Without blood, vampire bats cannot survive. Without a meal, they will die within two days. Scary? Vampire bats do not harm the animals. They just want a little blood each night!

Vampire bat

Describe how a vampire bat eats.**1** Why doesn't it hurt the animal?**2**

94

COMPREHENDING AS YOU GO

① Understand: Describing (A vampire bat finds a sleeping animal and makes a small cut with its sharp teeth. Then it laps up the blood.)

② Analyze: Drawing Conclusions (It's a very small cut. If the bat hurt the animal, the animal would wake up and chase the bat away . . .)

INCREDIBLE FLYING MACHINE

Superb flying machines!
Bats are the best of all.

With amazing grace,
They weave and dive
To find their food.

Throughout the world,
Bats are the best of all.

95

★ = New in this unit

MAIN IDEA AND SUPPORTING DETAILS

COMPREHENSION PROCESSES

Remember, Apply, Create

WRITING TRAITS

Conventions—Complete Sentence, Capital, Period

Identifying—Topic

Using Graphic Organizer
Explaining—Supporting Details
Generating—Main Idea

PROCEDURES

For each step, demonstrate and guide practice, as needed. Then have students complete the page independently.

1. **Topic: Answering Questions— Basic Instructions** (Item 1)
   - Have students read the top paragraph.
   - Have students read the question and write the topic in the blank.

2. **Supporting Details: Hierarchy Chart—Basic Instructions** (Item 2)
   Have students fill in the blanks to complete the supporting details.

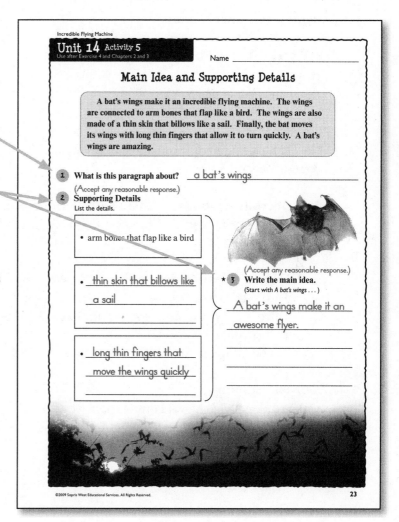

★3. **Main Idea: Hierarchy Chart, Sentence Writing—Basic Instructions** (Item 3)
   - Have students write a main idea sentence. Remind them to use a capital and a period. A main idea can be stated in different ways. Say something like:
     When you write the main idea, be sure to write a complete sentence. Start with the topic.
     What was the topic in this paragraph? (a bat's wings)
     What was the important thing you learned about a bat's wings? (A bat's wings make it an incredible flying machine.)
     So one way to say the main idea would be, "A bat's wings make it an incredible flying machine."
     You could also say, "A bat's wings make it an awesome flyer."
     What else could you say? A bat's wings . . . (are incredible).

   - Have students check and correct.
     Let's see if all the details support the main idea. The first detail is that bat wings have arm bones that flap like a bird. Does that detail make the bat an incredible flying machine? (yes)
     Does it make the wings awesome? (yes)
     Repeat with each detail.

   Note: A main idea can be stated in a variety of ways.

PASSAGE COMPREHENSION

COMPREHENSION PROCESSES
Remember, Understand

WRITING TRAITS
Organization—Sequence
Conventions—Period

PROCEDURES

For each step, demonstrate and guide practice, as needed. Then have students complete the page independently.

1. **Selection Response—Basic Instructions** (Items 1, 2)
   Have students read the question, then fill in the bubble and/or blank with the correct answer.

2. **Diagram: Description, Paragraph Writing—Specific Instructions** (Items 3, 4)
   • Have students read the directions and look at the diagram.
   • Have students write a paragraph that describes and sequences how a bat uses echolocation to locate food.
   • Guide students through the activity, only as needed.

Self-monitoring
Have students check and correct their work.

Defining and Using Vocabulary—locate

Defining Locating Information

Using Graphic Organizer, Viewing

Sequencing Describing Sentence Writing

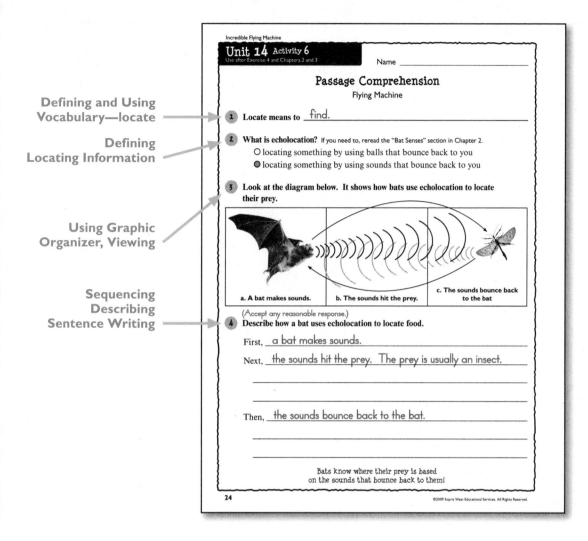

Incredible Flying Machine

Unit 14 Activity 6
Use after Exercise 4 and Chapters 2 and 3

Name _____

Passage Comprehension
Flying Machine

1 **Locate means to** _find._

2 **What is echolocation?** If you need to, reread the "Bat Senses" section in Chapter 2.
   ○ locating something by using balls that bounce back to you
   ● locating something by using sounds that bounce back to you

3 **Look at the diagram below. It shows how bats use echolocation to locate their prey.**

a. A bat makes sounds.   b. The sounds hit the prey.   c. The sounds bounce back to the bat

(Accept any reasonable response.)

4 **Describe how a bat uses echolocation to locate food.**

First, _a bat makes sounds._

Next, _the sounds hit the prey. The prey is usually an insect._
_____
_____

Then, _the sounds bounce back to the bat._
_____
_____

Bats know where their prey is based
on the sounds that bounce back to them!

24

① SOUND REVIEW

Use selected Sound Cards from Units 1–14.

PACING

Exercise 5a should take about 10 minutes, allowing about 10 minutes for the Focus Lesson.

② ACCURACY AND FLUENCY BUILDING

- For each task, have students say any underlined part, then read the word.
- Set a pace. Then have students read the whole words in each task and column.
- Provide repeated practice, building accuracy first, then fluency.

B1. Rhyming Words

Have students read each word set and identify what's the same about them.

E1. Tricky Words

- For each Tricky Word, have students use the sounds and word parts they know to silently sound out the word. Use the word in a sentence to help with pronunciation.
- If the word is unfamiliar, tell students the word.

lose	You can't always win. Sometimes you . . . *lose.*
losing	The Red Team was behind. They were . . . *losing.*
cycle	All plants and animals have a life . . . *cycle.*
suited	Stella looked nice in her dress. The color . . . *suited* . . . her.
heart	The organ that pumps blood through your body is the . . . *heart.*
tongues	Snakes have long, forked . . . *tongues.*
southern	The opposite of northern is . . . *southern.*
especially	I like to eat fruit . . . *especially* . . . apples.

- Have students go back and read the whole words in the column.

③ MULTISYLLABIC WORDS

For each word, have students read the syllables, then the whole word. Use the word in a sentence, as appropriate.

nocturnal	An animal that is active at night is . . . *nocturnal.*
superb	The chocolate cake was . . . *superb.*
shallow	The water wasn't deep. It was . . . *shallow.*
company	Jason started his own toy . . . *company.*
remarkable	The circus performers did . . . *remarkable* . . . stunts.
importance	The rules were listed in order of . . . *importance.*

④ MORPHOGRAPHS AND AFFIXES

- Have students read the underlined part, then the word.
- Repeat practice with whole words, mixing group and individual turns. Build accuracy, then fluency.

⑤ GENERALIZATION: READING NEW WORDS IN PARAGRAPHS

- Have students read the paragraph silently, then out loud. Tell students to use the sounds and word parts they know to read any difficult words.
- Repeat practice, as needed.

Incredible Flying Machine

Unit 14 Exercise 5a
Use before Chapter 4

1. **SOUND REVIEW** Use selected Sound Cards from Units 1–14.

2. **ACCURACY/FLUENCY BUILDING** For each column, have students say any underlined part, then read each word. Next, have them read the column.

A1 Mixed Practice	B1 Rhyming Words	C1 Related Words	D1 Word Endings	E1 Tricky Words
r<u>oo</u>sts	mate	locate	<u>shrinking</u>	lose
p<u>ow</u>der	rate	location	<u>beetles</u>	losing
w<u>ea</u>ther	migrate	echolocation	<u>warmer</u>	
creep<u>y</u>				cycle
A2 Compound Words	kind	pollen	breathe	suited
	mind	pollinate	breathing	heart
daytime	blind	pollinating		tongues
farmland			hibernate	southern
newborn			hibernation	especially

3. **MULTISYLLABIC WORDS** Have students read each word part, then read each whole word.

Ⓐ	noc•tur•nal	nocturnal	su•perb	superb
Ⓑ	shal•low	shallow	com•pa•ny	company
Ⓒ	re•mark•a•ble	remarkable	im•por•tance	importance

4. **MORPHOGRAPHS AND AFFIXES** Have students read each underlined part, then the word.

suscept<u>ible</u>	popula<u>tions</u>	suprising<u>ly</u>	<u>ex</u>tinction

5. **GENERALIZATION** Have students read the paragraph silently, then out loud. (New words: common, jacket, approaches, active)

Ants and wasps have many things in common. Likes ants, there are thousands of different types of wasps. One type of wasp is the yellow jacket. Just like ants, yellow jackets live in colonies.

Unlike ants, yellow jackets cannot survive in cold areas. As winter approaches, the workers die of cold, and the queen leaves to find shelter. In the spring, the queen becomes active and builds a new colony.

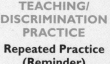

MASTERY TEACHING/ DISCRIMINATION PRACTICE

Repeated Practice (Reminder)

Provide repeated practice on each task. If you hear an error, gently correct the whole group with a demonstration and/or guided practice. Move to another skill or task, then return to the difficult item many times—mixing group and individual turns, independent of your voice. When a task is easy, build speed of recognition.

Remember, practice makes perfect! And practice builds fluency.

19

FACT SUMMARY

FOCUS LESSON
Skills and Strategies

PURPOSE

The purpose of this lesson is to provide explicit instruction in how to use notes to write a fact summary. The lesson prepares students for Comprehension and Skill Work. Students do not write in their books.

PREP NOTES

To demonstrate how to write a fact summary, use an overhead of page 20 in student *Exercise Book 3*, write on a transparency placed over the page, or use a paper copy.

COMPREHENSION PROCESSES

Remember, Understand, Create

PACING

Exercise 5b should take about 10 minutes.

PROCEDURES

❶ INTRODUCTION

Identifying—Topic, Fact; Defining and Using Vocabulary—endangered

Explain the purpose of the lesson. Say something like:

Remember, a fact summary is a great strategy for remembering and understanding interesting information. Look at your Focus Lesson. It shows a chart that we can use to write down and remember what we learned about bumblebee bats. This chart has been filled out for us. Read the topic. (the bumblebee bat)

Now, let's review the facts that we learned about this little bat.

Look at the first fact box. What did we learn about the bumblebee bat?

(It's the smallest bat in the world. Its wings are six inches wide.)

Repeat with each fact box.

❷ WRITING A FACT SUMMARY

Identifying—Topic; Using Vocabulary—endangered; Generating Ideas; Word Choice

- Guide writing a topic sentence. Say something like:

  Now we can use the chart to write a fact summary about bumblebee bats.

  We always start with a topic sentence. The topic sentence tells what our paragraph will be about.

  We can start with the topic and then write an interesting sentence.

  We could say, "The bumblebee bat is small."

  That sentence is a little dull. I think I'll make it more interesting by adding something more about the bat's size. I could write, "The smallest bat is the bumblebee bat."

  That's still a little dull. What else could we add? (It's the smallest bat in the world.)

  That's much better.

  Write "The smallest bat in the world is the bumblebee bat."

  Everyone, read the topic sentence. (The smallest bat in the world is the bumblebee bat.)

  That's a great topic sentence. It tells us what the paragraph will . . . (be about).

- Demonstrate and guide selecting and writing the facts.

  Now we need to write facts about the topic. Look at the boxes.

  We've already used the information about the bumblebee bat being the smallest bat.

  What else could we include? (It has wings that are six inches wide.)

  Let's start with "A bumblebee bat . . . "

  After the word "Fact," write "A bumblebee bat has wings that are only six inches wide."

- Have students review the remaining facts and select or combine facts to complete the fact summary.

  Write something like: "It has big ears and a pig-like nose. The bumblebee bat is endangered. There are only 130 of these small carnivores left in the world."

3 CHECK AND CORRECT

Have students read the paragraph and assist as you check and correct the paragraph.

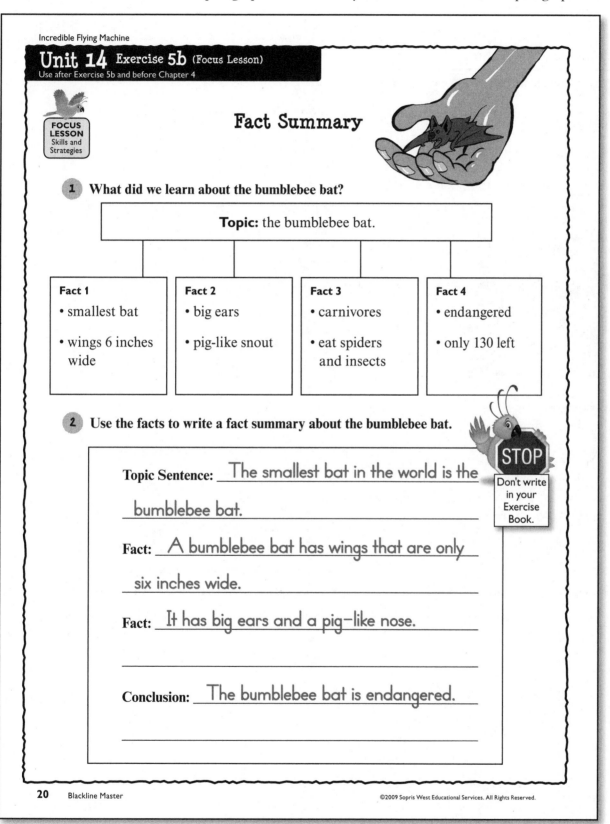

Incredible Flying Machine

Unit 14 Exercise 5b (Focus Lesson)
Use after Exercise 5b and before Chapter 4

FOCUS LESSON
Skills and Strategies

Fact Summary

1 What did we learn about the bumblebee bat?

Topic: the bumblebee bat.

Fact 1	**Fact 2**	**Fact 3**	**Fact 4**
• smallest bat	• big ears	• carnivores	• endangered
• wings 6 inches wide	• pig-like snout	• eat spiders and insects	• only 130 left

2 Use the facts to write a fact summary about the bumblebee bat.

Topic Sentence: The smallest bat in the world is the bumblebee bat.

Fact: A bumblebee bat has wings that are only six inches wide.

Fact: It has big ears and a pig-like nose.

Conclusion: The bumblebee bat is endangered.

STOP
Don't write in your Exercise Book.

COMPREHENSION PROCESSES

Understand, Apply, Analyze

PROCEDURES

Introducing Vocabulary

★ **common** ★ **nocturnal** ★ **roost, pollen**

- For each vocabulary word, have students read the word by parts, then read the whole word.
- Read the student-friendly explanations to students as they follow with their fingers. Then have students use the vocabulary word by following the gray text.
- Review and discuss the photos and illustrations.

"The key to a successful vocabulary program is to use both formal and informal encounters so that attention to vocabulary is happening any time and all the time" (McKeown & Beck, p. 21, 2004).

Encourage students to use vocabulary words from *Read Well 2* throughout the day. Here are some suggestions for keeping words alive in your classroom.

Thumbs Up: When a student spontaneously uses a new vocabulary word, give the student a thumbs up.

Vocabulary Stars: Keep a list of vocabulary words on a bulletin board or chart. When you hear a student use a word, put his or her name and a star next to the word.

Rotate words from previous units in and out of practice.

Vocabulary Stars

nocturnal ★ Leah ★ Kelton

classify ★ Aref ★ Ranelle

obviously ★ Molly ★ Mychal

WITH THE TEACHER

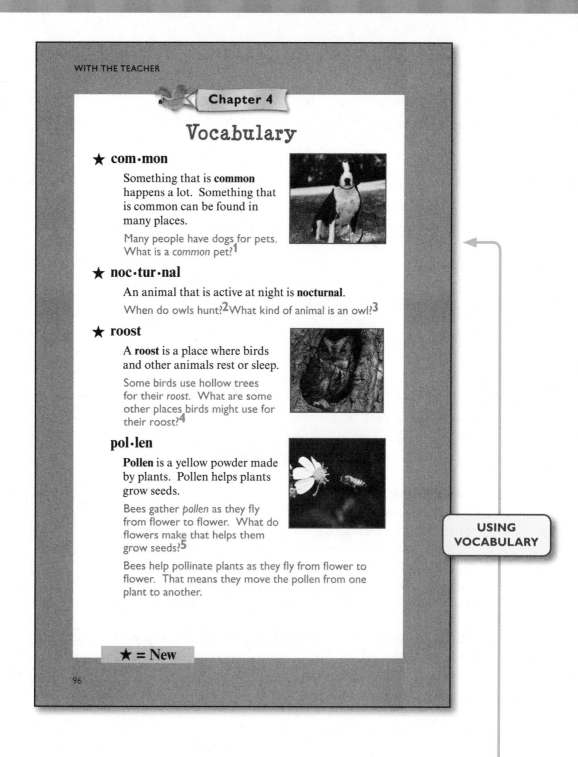

Chapter 4

Vocabulary

★ **com·mon**

Something that is **common** happens a lot. Something that is common can be found in many places.

Many people have dogs for pets. What is a *common* pet?[1]

★ **noc·tur·nal**

An animal that is active at night is **nocturnal**.

When do owls hunt?[2] What kind of animal is an owl?[3]

★ **roost**

A **roost** is a place where birds and other animals rest or sleep.

Some birds use hollow trees for their *roost*. What are some other places birds might use for their roost?[4]

pol·len

Pollen is a yellow powder made by plants. Pollen helps plants grow seeds.

Bees gather *pollen* as they fly from flower to flower. What do flowers make that helps them grow seeds?[5]

Bees help pollinate plants as they fly from flower to flower. That means they move the pollen from one plant to another.

★ = New

96

USING VOCABULARY

❶ **Understand:** Using Vocabulary—common (Dogs are common pets. Cats are common pets.)

❷ **Understand:** Explaining (Owls hunt at night.)

❸ **Analyze:** Classifying; **Apply:** Using Vocabulary—nocturnal (An owl is a nocturnal animal.)

❹ **Apply:** Using Vocabulary—roost (Birds might use a bird house for their roost.)

❺ **Understand:** Using Vocabulary—pollen (Flowers make pollen.)

CHAPTER 4 INSTRUCTIONS
Students read Chapter 4 with the teacher.

COMPREHENSION PROCESSES
Understand, Analyze

PROCEDURES

1. Reviewing Chapter 3

Explaining—Facts, Using Vocabulary—except

Have students turn to page 91. Quickly discuss the questions from Chapter 3, Setting a Purpose. Say something like:

Yesterday, you read Chapter 3 on your own. Let's see what you learned.

Where do bats live? (They live everywhere, except where it's too cold. They live in cities, in the country, in trees, in people's houses . . .)

What's the smallest bat? (The bumblebee bat is the smallest bat.)

What's the largest bat? (The flying fox is the largest bat.)

How does a vampire bat eat? (It bites sleeping animals and drinks their blood.)

2. Introducing Chapter 4

Identifying—Title

- Have students read the chapter title.
- Ask the gray text questions under the chapter title.

3. First Reading

- Ask questions and discuss the story as indicated by the gray text.
- Mix group and individual turns, independent of your voice.
  Have students work toward a group accuracy goal of 0–6 errors.
  Quietly keep track of errors made by all students in the group.
- After reading the story, practice any difficult words.
  Reread the story if students have not reached the accuracy goal.

4. Second Reading, Short Passage Practice: Developing Prosody

- Demonstrate expressive, fluent reading of the first two paragraphs.
- Guide practice with your voice.
- Provide individual turns while others track with their fingers and whisper read.
- Repeat with one paragraph at a time.

> **CORRECTING DECODING ERRORS**
>
> During story reading, gently correct any error, then have students reread the sentence.

5. Partner or Whisper Reading: Repeated Reading

 Before beginning independent work, have students finger track and partner or whisper read.

6. Comprehension and Skill Work

Tell students they will do Comprehension and Skill Activities 7 and 8 after they read Chapter 4. Guide practice, as needed. For teacher directions, see pages 90 and 91.

7. Homework 5: Repeated Reading

INCREDIBLE FLYING MACHINE

Chapter 4

Little Brown Bats

Why do you think the author included a whole chapter about little brown bats?[1]
Look at the headers. What do you think you will learn about little brown bats?[2]

Little Flying and Eating Machines

The most common bat in North America is the little brown bat. These flying machines are found all the way from southern Alaska to Mexico and across Canada and the United States.

Little Brown Bat

Of course, little brown bats have brown fur. Their wingspan is about eight to ten inches. They have small ears and 38 sharp little teeth—all the better to catch insects with.

Little brown bats are eating machines. These carnivores eat moths, wasps, beetles, and mosquitoes. A little brown bat can eat 1,200 mosquitoes in just one hour! For their small size, they eat an enormous amount of food. You would have to eat about 240 apples in one day to eat as much as a brown bat.

What bat are you most likely to see? Why?[3] Name two interesting facts about little brown bats.[4]

97

COMPREHENDING AS YOU GO

❶ **Analyze:** Drawing Conclusions (Little brown bats must be important. Little brown bats must be very interesting. Maybe there are little brown bats where the author lives . . .)

❷ **Apply:** Using Headings, Inferring; **Understand:** Using Vocabulary—colony, life cycle (We will learn what little brown bats eat, what their colonies are like, how they hibernate, what their life cycle is like, and why they are important.)

❸ **Apply:** Inferring; Explaining; Using Vocabulary—common (We are most likely to see a little brown bat because it is the most common bat in North America.)

❹ **Understand:** Summarizing—Facts (Little brown bats have 38 sharp little teeth. They can eat 1,200 mosquitoes in just an hour . . .)

Colonies

Some bats live alone, but little brown bats like company and live in colonies. As many as 1,000 bats may live in one cave. Like most bats, little brown bats are nocturnal. This means they are active at night.

Two to three hours after the sun sets, the little brown bats swarm from their daytime roosts. They hunt for two to three hours. By dawn, the little brown bats return. During the day, they hang upside down in their roost. They spend the day sleeping and cleaning themselves. They use their claws to groom their fur, and they use their tongues and teeth to clean their wings.

What makes a bat *nocturnal?***1** What do little brown bats do during the day?**2**

98

**COMPREHENDING
AS YOU GO**

❶ **Understand:** Explaining; Defining and Using Vocabulary—nocturnal (A bat is nocturnal because it is active at night.)

❷ **Understand:** Explaining (During the day, little brown bats sleep and clean themselves.)

INCREDIBLE FLYING MACHINE

Hibernation

Little brown bats live where winters are cold. As winter approaches, they fly to warmer places. Then the bats hibernate through the winter. This means they go into a sleep-like state. They do not hunt or eat. Their heart rate slows down, and they rest.

Life Cycle

In the spring, a mother bat gives birth to just one young pup. Newborn bats have no hair and are blind. They are cared for by their mother. In four weeks, they are adult size and have learned to fly. Little brown bats have surprisingly long lives. As far as scientists know, they can live as long as 33 years.

Describe what happens to a bat when it hibernates. [1]

99

COMPREHENDING
AS YOU GO

1 Understand: Describing, Summarizing—Facts (When a bat hibernates, it goes into a sleep-like state. Its heart slows down, and it rests. It does not hunt or eat.)

WITH THE TEACHER

The Importance of Bats

Scary? Creepy? Now that you know about bats, what do you think about them? Bats are important to habitats all over the world. Some pollinate flowers. Some eat insects. They are important to forests, farmland, and deserts. Bats are especially important to rain forests.

Bat populations throughout the world are shrinking because they are losing their habitats. Some bats are even endangered. Bats may become extinct because they give birth to so few babies. Who knows what would happen without these remarkable mammals!

What do you think would happen if bats became *extinct?*[1]

100

COMPREHENDING
AS YOU GO

❶ Analyze: Drawing Conclusions; **Apply:** Using Vocabulary—destroy (If bats became extinct, there would be more mosquitoes and other insects. The insects would destroy food crops. Without bats, there would be fewer flowers . . .)

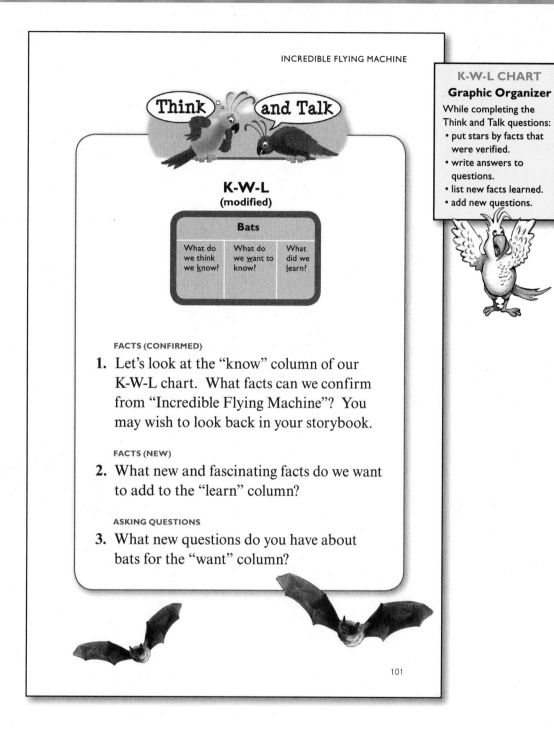

INCREDIBLE FLYING MACHINE

Think and Talk

K-W-L
(modified)

Bats		
What do we think we <u>k</u>now?	What do we <u>w</u>ant to know?	What did we <u>l</u>earn?

FACTS (CONFIRMED)

1. Let's look at the "know" column of our K-W-L chart. What facts can we confirm from "Incredible Flying Machine"? You may wish to look back in your storybook.

FACTS (NEW)

2. What new and fascinating facts do we want to add to the "learn" column?

ASKING QUESTIONS

3. What new questions do you have about bats for the "want" column?

101

K-W-L CHART
Graphic Organizer
While completing the Think and Talk questions:
- put stars by facts that were verified.
- write answers to questions.
- list new facts learned.
- add new questions.

❶ **Apply:** Locating Information; Verifying—Facts; Using Vocabulary—mammal, nocturnal (Bats are mammals. Bats are nocturnal—they do come out at night.)

❷ **Understand:** Locating Information; Summarizing—Facts; Using Vocabulary—mammal, echo, locate, prey, common, habitat (Bats are the only mammals that can fly. Bats have a hand-wing that is like a sail. Bats can change direction quickly. Bats use echoes to locate their prey. Bats live all over the world. There are 1,100 types of bats. The smallest bat is the bumblebee bat. The largest bat is the flying fox. The most common bat is the little brown bat. Bats are important to habitats all over the world . . .)

❸ **Create:** Generating Ideas, Asking Questions; **Apply:** Using Vocabulary—extinct (What can we do to keep bats from becoming extinct . . .)

PASSAGE READING FLUENCY

FLUENCY

Accuracy, Expression, Rate

PROCEDURES

For each step, demonstrate and guide practice, as needed. Then have students complete the page independently.

Passage Reading—Basic Instructions

- Have students read the practice words.
- Have students finger track and whisper read the story two times—the first time for accuracy and the second time for expression. Have students cross out a bat each time they finish.
- Have students do a one-minute Timed Reading and cross out the timer.

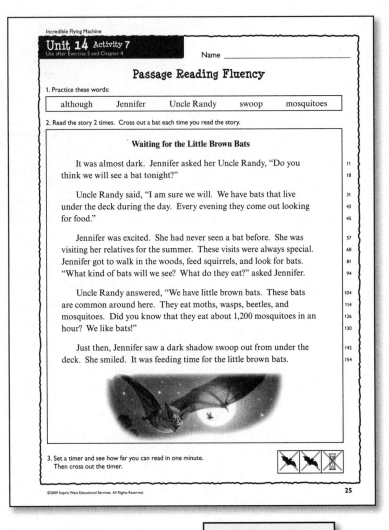

Incredible Flying Machine

Unit 14 Activity 7
Use after Exercise 5 and Chapter 4

Name _____

Passage Reading Fluency

1. Practice these words:

| although | Jennifer | Uncle Randy | swoop | mosquitoes |

2. Read the story 2 times. Cross out a bat each time you read the story.

Waiting for the Little Brown Bats

It was almost dark. Jennifer asked her Uncle Randy, "Do you think we will see a bat tonight?" | 11 / 18

Uncle Randy said, "I am sure we will. We have bats that live under the deck during the day. Every evening they come out looking for food." | 31 / 43 / 45

Jennifer was excited. She had never seen a bat before. She was visiting her relatives for the summer. These visits were always special. Jennifer got to walk in the woods, feed squirrels, and look for bats. "What kind of bats will we see? What do they eat?" asked Jennifer. | 57 / 68 / 81 / 94

Uncle Randy answered, "We have little brown bats. These bats are common around here. They eat moths, wasps, beetles, and mosquitoes. Did you know that they eat about 1,200 mosquitoes in an hour? We like bats!" | 104 / 114 / 126 / 130

Just then, Jennifer saw a dark shadow swoop out from under the deck. She smiled. It was feeding time for the little brown bats. | 142 / 154

3. Set a timer and see how far you can read in one minute.
   Then cross out the timer.

25

FACT SUMMARY • LOCATING INFORMATION

COMPREHENSION PROCESSES

Understand

WRITING TRAITS

Ideas and Content
Organization—Topic Sentence,
Supporting Details
Word Choice
Conventions—Complete Sentence,
Capital, Period
Presentation

Using Graphic Organizer
Locating Information; Identifying—
Supporting Details/Facts

Summarizing—Main Idea/Topic
Supporting Details/Facts
Sentence Writing

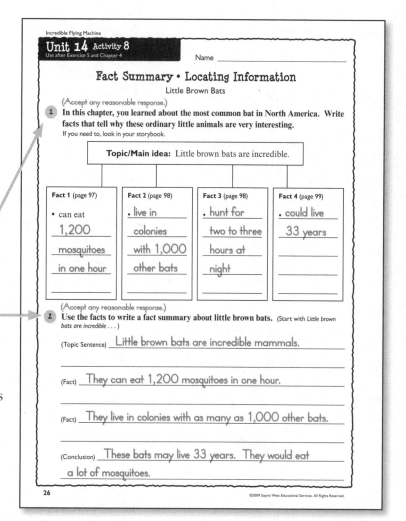

Incredible Flying Machine

Unit 14 Activity 8
Use after Exercise 5 and Chapter 4

Name _____

Fact Summary • Locating Information
Little Brown Bats

(Accept any reasonable response.)

1 In this chapter, you learned about the most common bat in North America. Write facts that tell why these ordinary little animals are very interesting.
If you need to, look in your storybook.

Topic/Main idea: Little brown bats are incredible.

Fact 1 (page 97)
• can eat
1,200
mosquitoes
in one hour

Fact 2 (page 98)
. live in
colonies
with 1,000
other bats

Fact 3 (page 98)
. hunt for
two to three
hours at
night

Fact 4 (page 99)
. could live
33 years

(Accept any reasonable response.)

2 Use the facts to write a fact summary about little brown bats. (Start with *Little brown bats are incredible . . .*)

(Topic Sentence) Little brown bats are incredible mammals.

(Fact) They can eat 1,200 mosquitoes in one hour.

(Fact) They live in colonies with as many as 1,000 other bats.

(Conclusion) These bats may live 33 years. They would eat a lot of mosquitoes.

26

©2009 Sopris West Educational Services. All Rights Reserved.

PROCEDURES

For each step, demonstrate and guide practice, as needed. Then have students complete the page independently.

1. **Main Idea/Supporting Details: Hierarchy Chart—Specific Instructions** (Item 1)
   - Have students read the topic/main idea.
   - Have students write and complete the facts that explain how little brown bats are incredible.
     This activity has a main idea chart, just like our Focus Lesson.
     The top box shows the main idea. It starts with the topic.
     What's the topic? (little brown bats)
     What's the main idea about little brown bats? (They are incredible.)

     The boxes under the main idea show the facts or details that tell us what makes a little brown bat incredible. You're going to look in your storybook to complete this activity.
     Some of the facts are started for you. Look at Fact 1. Where will you look in your storybook to complete that fact? (page 97)
     Remember, you don't have to write complete sentences. You can write phrases.

2. **Fact Summary: Paragraph Writing—Specific Instructions**
   Have students write a fact summary paragraph with the facts from Item 1. Assist, only as needed.

Self-monitoring
Have students check and correct their work.

❶ SOUND REVIEW

Have students read the sounds in each row. Work for accuracy, then fluency.

❷ ACCURACY AND FLUENCY BUILDING

- For each task, have students say any underlined part, then read the word.
- Set a pace. Then have students read the whole words in each task and column.
- Provide repeated practice, building accuracy first, then fluency.

B1. Bossy E

Have students identify the underlined sound and then read the word.

C1. Multisyllabic Words

- For the list of words divided by syllables, have students read each syllable, then the whole word. Use the word in a sentence, as appropriate.
- For the list of whole words, build accuracy and then fluency.

always	Judith says "phooey" all the time. She . . . *always* . . . says it.
belly	The snake slithered along on its . . . *belly*.
hurry	"We're late," Mom said. "You need to . . . *hurry*."
return	Please give the quarter back. Please . . . *return* . . . it.
cozy	The bedroom slippers looked warm and . . . *cozy*.
insects	Ants, beetles, and flies are . . . *insects*.
baby	That's the smallest ant I've ever seen. Maybe it's a . . . *baby* . . . ant.

D1. Tricky Words

- For each Tricky Word, have students use the sounds and word parts they know to silently sound out the word. Use the word in a sentence to help with pronunciation.
- If the word is unfamiliar, tell students the word.

comes	We need to be at the bus stop when the bus . . . *comes*.
search	When the trophy was lost, the community helped . . . *search* . . . for it.
where	Jerod was lost. He didn't know . . . *where* . . . he was.
mother	The little bird fell out of its nest and couldn't find its . . . *mother*.

- Have students go back and read the whole words in the column.

❸ WORDS IN CONTEXT

For each word, have students use the sounds and word parts they know to silently sound out the word. Then have students read the sentence. Assist, as needed.

❹ MORPHOGRAPHS AND AFFIXES

- Have students read the underlined part, then the word.
- Repeat practice with whole words, mixing group and individual turns. Build accuracy, then fluency.

Fluency

Unit 14 Exercise 6
Use before A Bat's Life

1. SOUND REVIEW Have students review sounds for accuracy, then for fluency.

Ⓐ	ew	ph	au	gi	oi
Ⓑ	ue	u_e	igh	o_e	ir

2. ACCURACY/FLUENCY BUILDING For each column, have students say any underlined part, then read each word. Next, have them read the column.

A1 **Mixed Practice**	**B1** **Bossy E**	**C1** **Multisyllabic Words**		**D1** **Tricky Words**
bul<u>ge</u>	c<u>a</u>ve	al•ways	always	comes
chi<u>ll</u>	br<u>a</u>ve	bel•ly	belly	search
spr<u>i</u>ng	w<u>a</u>ke	hur•ry	hurry	where
sn<u>u</u>g	sn<u>a</u>kes	re•turn	return	mother
<u>a</u>lone	**B2** **Related Words**	co•zy	cozy	
sw<u>ee</u>t	hunt	in•sects	insects	
<u>ow</u>ls	hunted	ba•by	baby	
gr<u>ow</u>n	hunting			

ENTHUSIASM!
Small accomplishments become big accomplishments with your enthusiasm.

3. WORDS IN CONTEXT Have students use the sounds and word parts they know to figure out each word. Then have them read each sentence.

Ⓐ	e•cho	I could hear my voice <u>echo</u> in the tunnel.
Ⓑ	jui•cy	The peach was ripe and <u>juicy</u>.

4. MORPHOGRAPHS AND AFFIXES Have students read the underlined part, then the word.

Ⓐ	collect<u>ible</u>	vis<u>ible</u>	incred<u>ible</u>	suscept<u>ible</u>
Ⓑ	natur<u>al</u>	nerv<u>ous</u>	<u>dis</u>play	cup<u>ful</u>

21

FLUENCY PASSAGE INSTRUCTIONS

This Story Reading targets fluency as the primary goal of instruction and practice. Students do repeated readings of this poem to improve accuracy, expression, and rate.

PROCEDURES

1. Warm-Up: Partner Reading or Whisper Reading

Before beginning group Story Reading, have students finger track and partner or whisper read the selection.

2. First Reading

- Mix group and individual turns, independent of your voice. Have students work toward a group accuracy goal of 0–2 errors. Quietly keep track of errors made by all students in the group.
- After reading the story, practice any difficult words. Reread the story if students have not reached the accuracy goal.

3. Second Reading, Short Passage Practice: Developing Prosody

- Demonstrate reading the first stanza with expression and fluency. Have students finger track as you read.
- Have students choral read the first stanza. Encourage reading with expression and fluency.
- Repeat with second stanza.

> **PARTNER READING— CHECKOUT OPPORTUNITY**
>
> While students are Partner Reading, listen to individuals read the passage. Work on accuracy and fluency, as needed.

4. Third Reading, Group Timed Readings: Repeated Reading

- Select a page. Encourage each child to work for a personal best. Have students whisper read for a one-minute Timed Reading. Tell students to go back to the top of the page and keep reading until the minute is up.
- Have students put their finger on the last word they read and count the number of words read correctly in one minute.
- Have students do a Second Timed Reading of the same page.
- Have students try to beat their last score.
- Celebrate improvements.

5. Written Assessment (Comprehension and Skill)

Tell students they will do a Written Assessment after they read "A Bat's Life." (For teacher directions, see pages 97–99.)

6. Homework 6: Repeated Reading

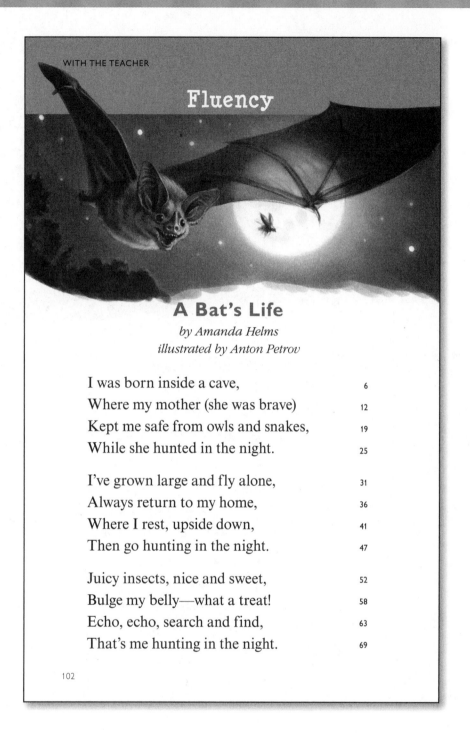

WITH THE TEACHER

Fluency

A Bat's Life

by Amanda Helms
illustrated by Anton Petrov

I was born inside a cave,	6
Where my mother (she was brave)	12
Kept me safe from owls and snakes,	19
While she hunted in the night.	25
I've grown large and fly alone,	31
Always return to my home,	36
Where I rest, upside down,	41
Then go hunting in the night.	47
Juicy insects, nice and sweet,	52
Bulge my belly—what a treat!	58
Echo, echo, search and find,	63
That's me hunting in the night.	69

102

A BAT'S LIFE

Make a scent, catch a mate.	6
Hurry now, it's getting late.	11
In the spring, I'll have a pup.	18
She'll go hunting in the night.	24
Winter comes, the air is chill.	30
But my belly's had its fill.	36
Now I'll sleep, snug and cozy.	42
No more hunting in the night.	48
Spring is here, and so I wake,	55
Fly for bugs by a lake.	61
Soon I'll have my baby pup,	67
We'll go hunting in the night.	73

103

WRITTEN ASSESSMENT (1 of 3)

COMPREHENSION PROCESSES

Remember, Understand, Apply, Analyze

WRITING TRAITS

Conventions—Complete Sentence, Beginning Capital, Period
Presentation

Test Taking →

Unit 14 Written Assessment
Use after Exercise 6 and A Bat's Life

WARM-UP

| nursery | mosquitoes | billowy | ceiling | special |

Growing Up as a Little Brown Bat

I'm a little brown bat. When I was born, I had no hair on my body. I couldn't see because my eyes were closed. I stayed real close to my mother. When she went hunting, I hung onto her tightly as she sailed through the night air grabbing mosquitoes.

My eyes opened two days after I was born. I saw that I was in a dark cave with thousands of other mothers and baby bats. It was a bat nursery! Soon I was old enough to stay with the other baby bats while my mother went hunting. She and I had special calls so we could find each other when she returned.

I drank my mother's milk and grew fast. When I was four weeks old, I was as big as she was. One day I let go of the ceiling and flapped my billowy wings. I could fly! My mother showed me how to catch insects. Soon I was able to take care of myself.

continued →

104

WRITTEN ASSESSMENT (2 of 3)

Identifying—Topic Sentence Completion

Identifying—Facts; Note Taking

Using Vocabulary—mammals

Identifying—Supporting Details

Using Vocabulary—carnivores

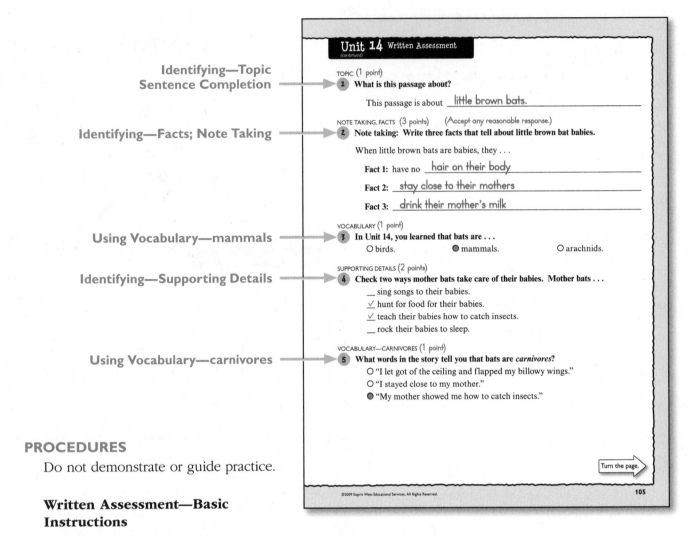

Unit 14 Written Assessment
(continued)

TOPIC (1 point)

1 **What is this passage about?**

This passage is about   little brown bats.

NOTE TAKING, FACTS (3 points)   (Accept any reasonable response.)

2 **Note taking: Write three facts that tell about little brown bat babies.**

When little brown bats are babies, they . . .

Fact 1: have no   hair on their body

Fact 2:   stay close to their mothers

Fact 3:   drink their mother's milk

VOCABULARY (1 point)

3 **In Unit 14, you learned that bats are . . .**
- ○ birds.
- ● mammals.
- ○ arachnids.

SUPPORTING DETAILS (2 points)

4 **Check two ways mother bats take care of their babies. Mother bats . . .**
- __ sing songs to their babies.
- ✓ hunt for food for their babies.
- ✓ teach their babies how to catch insects.
- __ rock their babies to sleep.

VOCABULARY—CARNIVORES (1 point)

5 **What words in the story tell you that bats are _carnivores_?**
- ○ "I let got of the ceiling and flapped my billowy wings."
- ○ "I stayed close to my mother."
- ● "My mother showed me how to catch insects."

Turn the page.

105

PROCEDURES

Do not demonstrate or guide practice.

Written Assessment—Basic Instructions

1. Introduce the Written Assessment.
   - Tell students that their work today is an opportunity for them to show what they can do independently. Say something like:
     You should be very proud of your accomplishments. Remember, on a Written Assessment, you get to show me what you can do all by yourself.

   - Tell students they will whisper read the passage and then answer the questions without help.

2. Check for student understanding.
   Say something like:
   Look at your assessment. What are you going to do first? (write my name)

   What are going to do next? (whisper read the passage)
   What will you do after you read the passage? (answer the questions)

   That's great. Now what will you do if you get to a hard question?
   (reread the question and try again)
   That's right. What should you do if it's still hard? (reread the passage and try again)
   Very good. And if you still aren't sure, what will you do? (do my best and keep going)

WRITTEN ASSESSMENT (3 of 3)

Sequencing; Identifying—Events
Sentence Completion

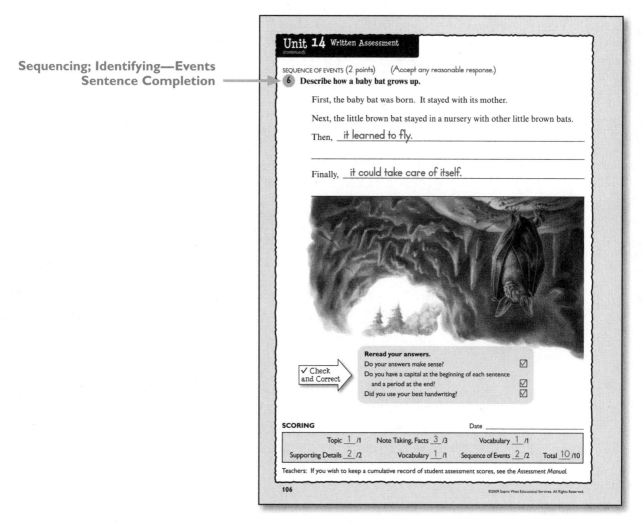

3. Remind students to check and correct.
   When you finish your assessment, what should you do? (check and correct)
   That's right. Go to the top of the page. Reread the questions and make sure your answers make sense. Fix anything that doesn't sound right. Make sure you have an answer for every question.

4. Remind students what to do when they finish their work.

End of the Unit

In this section, you will find:

Making Decisions

As you near the end of the unit, plan to give the Written Assessment and the Oral Reading Fluency Assessment to each child in your group. Use this section as a general guide for making instructional decisions and doing diagnostic planning.

Written Assessment

The Unit 14 Written Assessment is located on page 103 of *Activity Book 3* and on the CD.

Oral Reading Fluency Assessment

The Unit 14 Oral Reading Fluency Assessment is located on page 104 of this teacher's guide and in the *Assessment Manual*.

Certificate of Achievement

Celebrate your children's accomplishments. When your students master the unit skills, send home the Certificate of Achievement.

Extra Practice Lessons

Use the Extra Practice lessons for students who need additional decoding and fluency work. Student materials can be copied from the Extra Practice blackline masters.

Making Decisions

GENERAL ASSESSMENT GUIDELINES

1. After students read Story Reading 6, "A Bat's Life," give the group the Unit 14 Written Assessment in place of Comprehension and Skill Work. Follow the instructions on pages 97–99 of this guide.

2. While the group is completing the Written Assessment or any time during the day, administer the Oral Reading Fluency Assessment. Assess each student individually.

   Optional: Graph the results of the assessment. (See Unit 7 Teacher's Guide, pages 92 and 95.)
   • If the student's words correct per minute go up, congratulate the student.
   • If the student's words correct per minute go down, discuss the student's overall improvement and help him or her identify ways to improve for the next assessment.

3. Score oral fluency responses on the Student Assessment Record. Adhere to the scoring criteria in the *Assessment Manual.* Use a stopwatch to time how long it takes each student to read the Oral Reading Fluency Passage and record errors.

USING WRITTEN ASSESSMENT RESULTS

Results of the Written Assessment *should not* be used to determine whether a student or group of students continues forward in the program. As long as students pass the Oral Reading Fluency Assessment, they should continue forward with the next unit.

The Written Assessment should be used to informally monitor how well students read independently and answer questions in writing. If any student has difficulty with the Written Assessment, re-administer the assessment orally.

If the student has difficulty answering the questions orally:
• Record the types of errors (e.g., main idea, sequencing, open-ended response).
• Provide explicit instruction for these types of questions during reading group, before independent work, and in tutorials, as needed.
   1) Demonstrate (or model) appropriate responses, guide practice, and provide opportunities for independent practice.
   2) For inferential questions, think aloud with students—explain how you arrive at an answer.
   3) For literal questions, teach students to reread a passage, locate information, reread the question, and respond.

USING THE ORAL READING FLUENCY RESULTS

At the end of each unit, you will need to make decisions regarding student progress. Should students go forward in the program? Does the group need Extra Practice before proceeding? Do individuals require more assistance and practice to continue working in their group? These decisions all require use of the oral reading fluency data and professional judgment. As you analyze assessment results, watch for trends and anomalies.

See the *Assessment Manual* for detailed information and instructional recommendations. General guidelines and recommendations follow:

Strong Pass ≥ 115 WCPM 0–2 errors	• Continue with the current pace of instruction. • Have students set goals. (Until students are reading approximately 180 words correct per minute, oral reading fluency continues to be an instructional goal.)
Pass 94–114 WCPM 0–2 errors	• Continue with the current pace of instruction. Consider increasing fluency practice.
No Pass ≤ 93 WCPM	• If a child scores a No Pass but has previously passed all assessments, you may wish to advance the student to the next unit, then carefully monitor the student. • If a child scores a No Pass but has previously passed all assessments, you may wish to advance the student to the next unit and also provide additional practice opportunities. (See below.) • If a child scores two consecutive No Passes or periodic No Passes, additional practice must be provided. (See below.) • If a child scores three consecutive No Passes, the student should be placed in a lower-performing group.

RED FLAG
A No Pass is a red flag. A mild early intervention can prevent an intense and time-consuming intervention in the future.

Added Practice Options for Groups

Warm-Ups:
• Begin each lesson with Partner Reading of the previous day's homework.
• Begin each day with Partner Reading of a Word Fluency from Extra Practice.
• Begin each lesson with a five-minute Fluency Booster. Place copies of the Unit 7–13 *Read Well* Homework in three-ring notebooks. Each day, have students begin Finger Tracking and Whisper Reading at Unit 7, Homework 1. At the end of five minutes, have students mark where they are in their notebooks. The next day, the goal is to read farther.
• Begin each Story Reading with a review of the previous day's story.
• After reading the story, include Short Passage Practice on a daily basis.

Extended Units: If several children begin to score No Passes or barely pass, extend the unit by adding Extra Practices 1, 2, and/or 3. Extra Practice lessons include Decoding Practice, Fluency Passage, Word Fluency, and a Comprehension and Skill Activity. (See pages 106–116 in this guide.)

Jell-Well Reviews: A Jell-Well Review is the *Read Well* term for a review of earlier units. A Jell-Well Review is a period of time taken to celebrate what children have learned and an opportunity to firm up their foundation of learning. To complete a Jell-Well Review, take the group back to the last unit for which all students scored Strong Passes. Then quickly cycle back up. See the *Assessment Manual* for how to build a Jell-Well Review.

Added Practice Options for Individual Students

Tutorials: Set up five-minute tutorials on a daily basis with an assistant, trained volunteer, or cross-age tutor. Have the tutor provide Short Passage Practice and Timed Readings or Extra Practice lessons.

Double Dose: Find ways to provide a double dose of *Read Well* instruction.
- Have the student work in his or her group *and* a lower-performing group.
- Have an instructional assistant, older student, or parent volunteer preview or review lessons.
- Have an instructional assistant provide instruction with Extra Practice lessons.
- Preview new lessons or review previous lessons.

END-OF-THE-UNIT CELEBRATION

When students pass the Oral Reading Fluency Assessment, celebrate with the Certificate of Achievement on page 105.

Note: Using the Flesch-Kincaid Grade Level readability formula, the Unit 14 Assessment has a 2.7 readability level. Readabilities are based on number of words per sentence and number of syllables per word. Adding one or two multisyllabic words can increase readability by a month or two. Though we are attending to readability for the assessments, the overriding factor is decodability.

Especially Excellent

Jamal

successfully completed

Read Well 2 Unit 14 · Bats

with _125_ words correct per minute.

Teacher Signature _Mrs. Smith_

Date _Jan. 10_

TRICKY WORD and FOCUS SKILL WARM-UP

wondered	warmer	fruit	roosted	stomach	curious

ORAL READING FLUENCY PASSAGE

The Curious Bat

★Bob was a curious brown bat. The other bats in his 11
colony ate bugs, but Bob wondered what fruit tasted like. He 22
tried to eat an apple. It got stuck in his sharp teeth, and his 36
stomach hurt. Bob decided bugs were best. 43

The other bats roosted in the cave. Bob wondered what 53
it would be like to fly in the sunshine. Bob could hardly keep his 67
eyes open in the bright sun. He tried to find a nice moth to eat, 82
but they all hid from him. Bob decided the dark night was better 95
than a sunny day. 99

The other bats flew to a warmer place for the winter. Bob 111
wondered what winter was like. When it finally snowed, he 121
thought, "I'm very cold, and I miss my friends." So off he flew to 135
join the other bats in their new warm cave. 144

ORAL READING FLUENCY	Start timing at the ★. Mark errors. Make a single slash in the text (/) at 60 seconds. Have the student complete the passage. If the student completes the passage in less than 60 seconds, have the student go back to the ★ and continue reading. Make a double slash (//) in the text at 60 seconds.
WCPM	Determine words correct per minute by subtracting errors from words read in 60 seconds.
STRONG PASS	The student scores no more than 2 errors on the first pass through the passage and reads 115 or more words correct per minute. Proceed to Unit 15.
PASS	The student scores no more than 2 errors on the first pass through the passage and reads 94 to 114 words correct per minute. Proceed to Unit 15.
NO PASS	The student scores 3 or more errors on the first pass through the passage and/or reads 93 or fewer words correct per minute. Provide added fluency practice with RW2 Unit 14 Extra Practice. (Lessons follow the certificate at the end of the teacher's guide.) After completing the Extra Practice, retest the student.

Especially Excellent

_____

successfully completed

Read Well 2 Unit 14 • *Bats*

with _____ words correct per minute.

Teacher Signature _____

Date _____

Especially Excellent

_____

successfully completed

Read Well 2 Unit 14 • *Bats*

with _____ words correct per minute.

Teacher Signature _____

Date _____

PROCEDURES

1. Sound Review

Use selected Sound Cards from Units 1–14.

2. Sounding Out Smoothly

- For each word, have students say the underlined part, sound out the word smoothly, then read the whole word. Use the words in sentences, as needed.
- Have students read all the words in the row, building accuracy first, then fluency.
- Repeat practice. Mix group and individual turns, independent of your voice.

3. Accuracy and Fluency Building

- For each task, have students say any underlined part, then read each word.
- Set a pace. Then have students read the whole words in each task and column.
- Provide repeated practice, building accuracy first, then fluency.

4. Tricky Words

Have students read each row for accuracy, then fluency.

5. Multisyllabic Words

For each word, have students read each syllable out loud, then tell how many syllables are in the word. If needed, use the word in a sentence. Have students read the whole word.

6. Dictation

roost, join, house, grip, ship, trip

- Say "roost." Have students say the word. Have students touch or write the sounds, then read the word. Say something like:

  The first word is **roost.** Say the word. (roost)

  What's the first sound? (/rrr/) Touch under /rrr/.
  What's the next sound? (/ō͞o/) Write /ō͞o/ with the o-o pattern.
  What's the next sound? (/sss/) Touch under /sss/.
  What's the last sound? (/t/) Touch under /t/.
  Read the word. (roost)

- Repeat with "join" and "house."
- Continue with the rhyming words: grip, ship, trip.

Unit 14 Decoding Practice

Name _____

1. SOUND REVIEW Use selected Sound Cards from Units 1–14.

2. SOUNDING OUT SMOOTHLY Have students say the underlined part, sound out and read each word, then read the row.

thi<u>ck</u>	su<u>ch</u>	p<u>o</u>nd	sn<u>ow</u>

3. ACCURACY/FLUENCY BUILDING Have students say any underlined part, then read each word. Next, have students read the column.

A1 Mixed Review	**B1** Rhyming Words	**C1** Word Endings	**D1** Related Words
inches	br<u>ight</u>	<u>bump</u>y	value
insects	t<u>ight</u>	<u>hard</u>ly	valued
inside	l<u>ight</u>	<u>tast</u>ed	valuable
invite		**C2** Bossy E	**D2** Shifty Words
every	g<u>oo</u>d	th<u>e</u>se	b<u>a</u>t
river	w<u>oo</u>d	w<u>i</u>de	ba<u>ck</u>
winter	st<u>oo</u>d	p<u>o</u>le	bar<u>k</u>
mammals	pl<u>ace</u>	c<u>a</u>ve	<u>d</u>ark
common	sp<u>ace</u>	<u>a</u>te	<u>sh</u>ark
problem	tr<u>ace</u>		shar<u>p</u>

4. TRICKY WORDS Have students read each row for accuracy, then fluency.

neighbors	fruit	stomach	should	building	5
surface	people	only	wonder	warm	10

5. MULTISYLLABIC WORDS Have students read the word by parts, tell how many syllables are in the word, then read the whole word.

Ⓐ	cu•ri•ous	curious	col•o•ny	colony
Ⓑ	lo•ca•tion	location	A•mer•i•ca	America
Ⓒ	mos•qui•toes	mosquitoes	com•mu•ni•ty	community

6. DICTATION Say the word. Guide students as they say, finger count, and segment the word. Have students say each sound as they touch or write it.

A1 Vowels	**B1** Rhyming Words
r <u>oo</u> s t	g r <u>i</u> p
j <u>oi</u> n	sh <u>i</u> p
h <u>ou</u> s e	t r <u>i</u> p

PROCEDURES

1. First Reading

Mix group and individual turns, independent of your voice. Have students work toward an accuracy goal of 0–2 errors and practice any difficult words.

2. Second Reading, Short Passage Practice: Developing Prosody

- Demonstrate how to read a line or two with expression. Read at a rate slightly faster than the students' rate. Say something like:

  Listen as I read the first two sentences with expression and phrasing. I'm going to emphasize certain words and pause between sentences.

  "Little brown bats are common in North America. These mammals can be valuable neighbors."

- Guide practice with your voice. Now read the paragraph with me.

- Provide individual turns while others track with their fingers and whisper read. Provide descriptive and positive feedback.

  [Karta], you read with wonderful expression!

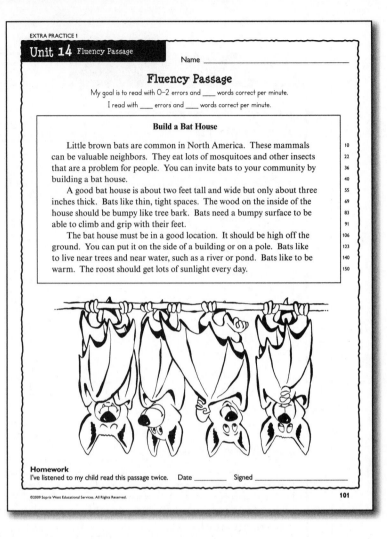

EXTRA PRACTICE 1

Unit 14 Fluency Passage

Name _____

Fluency Passage

My goal is to read with 0–2 errors and ____ words correct per minute.

I read with ____ errors and ____ words correct per minute.

Build a Bat House

    Little brown bats are common in North America. These mammals can be valuable neighbors. They eat lots of mosquitoes and other insects that are a problem for people. You can invite bats to your community by building a bat house.

    A good bat house is about two feet tall and wide but only about three inches thick. Bats like thin, tight spaces. The wood on the inside of the house should be bumpy like tree bark. Bats need a bumpy surface to be able to climb and grip with their feet.

    The bat house must be in a good location. It should be high off the ground. You can put it on the side of a building or on a pole. Bats like to live near trees and near water, such as a river or pond. Bats like to be warm. The roost should get lots of sunlight every day.

10 / 22 / 36 / 40 / 55 / 69 / 83 / 91 / 106 / 123 / 140 / 150

Homework
I've listened to my child read this passage twice. Date _____ Signed _____

101

3. Partner Reading: Repeated Reading (Checkout Opportunity)

While students do Partner Reading, listen to individuals read the passage. Work on accuracy and fluency, as needed.

4. Homework: Repeated Reading

Have students read the story at home.

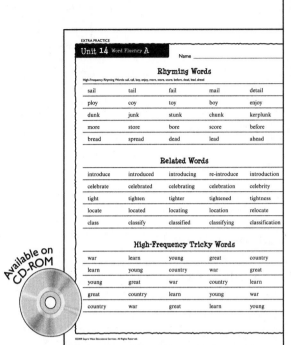

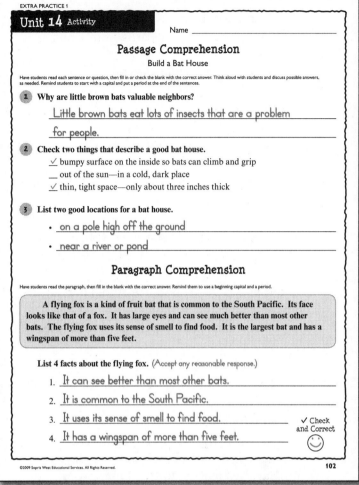

PROCEDURES

For each step, demonstrate and guide practice, as needed. Then have students complete the page independently.

1. Activity

Passage Comprehension

- Have students read each sentence or question, then fill in or check the blank with the correct answer.
- Think aloud with students and discuss the multiple-choice options, as needed.

Paragraph Comprehension

- Have students read the paragraph.
- Have students read each numbered sentence, then fill in the blanks with complete sentences.
- Have students read the completed sentences.

Self-monitoring

Have students read and check their work, then draw a happy face in the Check and Correct circle.

2. Word Fluency (BLMs are located on the CD.)

- To build fluency, have students read Rhyming Words, Related Words, and High-Frequency Tricky Words. Have students read each section three times in a row.
- To build accuracy, have students read all sets with partners.

ACCURACY BEFORE FLUENCY (Reminder)

Word Fluency is designed to build accuracy and fluency. Students should practice for accuracy before working on fluency.

PROCEDURES

1. Sound Review

Use selected Sound Cards from Units 1–14.

2. Sounding Out Smoothly

- For each word, have students say the underlined part, sound out the word smoothly, then read the whole word. Use the words in sentences, as needed.
- Have students read all the words in the row, building accuracy first, then fluency.
- Repeat practice. Mix group and individual turns, independent of your voice.

3. Accuracy and Fluency Building

- For each task, have students say any underlined part, then read each word.
- Set a pace. Then have students read the whole words in each task and column.
- Provide repeated practice, building accuracy first, then fluency.

4. Tricky Words

Have students read each row for accuracy, then fluency.

5. Multisyllabic Words

For each word, have students read each syllable out loud, then tell how many syllables are in the word. If needed, use the word in a sentence. Have students read the whole word.

6. Dictation

lunch, crunch, crunchy, bear hug, ladybug, earplug

- Say "lunch." Have students say the word. Have students touch or write the sounds, then read the word.

  The first word is *lunch.* Say the word. (lunch)

  What's the first sound? (/lll/) Touch under /lll/.
  What's the next sound? (/ŭŭŭ/) Write /ŭŭŭ/.
  What's the next sound? (/nnn/) Touch under /nnn/.
  What's the last sound? (/ch/) Touch under /ch/.
  Read the word. (lunch)

- Repeat with "crunch" and "crunchy."
- Continue with the rhyming words: bear hug, ladybug, earplug.

CAUTION

Your children may not need Extra Practice. Use assessment results to determine if Extra Practice is needed.

Unit 14 Decoding Practice

Name _____

1. SOUND REVIEW Use selected Sound Cards from Units 1–14.

2. SOUNDING OUT SMOOTHLY Have students say the underlined part, sound out and read each word, then read the row.

pr<u>ey</u>	w<u>i</u>ngs	fl<u>ew</u>	f<u>or</u>th

3. ACCURACY/FLUENCY BUILDING Have students say any underlined part, then read each word. Next, have students read the column.

A1 Sound Practice	**B1** Word Endings	**C1** Related Words	**D1** Contractions
b<u>a</u>by	try	billow	there's
l<u>a</u>dy	tried	billowed	you're
<u>o</u>pen	<u>fold</u>ed	billowing	we've
<u>o</u>ver	<u>snort</u>ed	protect	**D2** Tricky Words With Endings
c<u>o</u>zy	<u>decid</u>ed	protected	<u>wonder</u>ed
bel<u>ow</u>	<u>roost</u>ed	protection	<u>search</u>ing
wind<u>ow</u>	<u>click</u>ed	locate	<u>wear</u>ing
Bett<u>y</u>	<u>peek</u>ed	located	<u>warm</u>er
fuzz<u>y</u>	<u>napp</u>ed	location	

4. TRICKY WORDS Have students read each row for accuracy, then fluency.

other	his	was	would	from	5
thought	through	they	were	where	10

5. MULTISYLLABIC WORDS Have students read the word by parts, tell how many syllables are in the word, then read the whole word.

Ⓐ	whis•tled	whistled	bee•tles	beetles
Ⓑ	per•fect	perfect	pred•a•tors	predators
Ⓒ	fa•vor•ite	favorite	flex•i•ble	flexible

6. DICTATION Say the word. Guide students as they say and segment the word. Have students say each sound as they touch or write it.

A1 Shifty Words	**B1** Rhyming Words
l <u>u</u> n ch <u>c</u> <u>r</u> u n ch c r u n ch <u>y</u>	b ea r h <u>u g</u> l a d y b <u>u g</u> ea r p l <u>u g</u>

103

PROCEDURES

1. First Reading

Mix group and individual turns, independent of your voice. Have students work toward an accuracy goal of 0–2 errors and practice any difficult words.

2. Second Reading, Timed Reading: Repeated Reading

• Once the group accuracy goal has been achieved, time individual students for 30 or 60 seconds while the other children track with their fingers and whisper read.

• Determine words correct per minute. Record student scores. Celebrate when students reach their goals!

Wow! [Eli], you met your goal. That was your best score ever. You get to read to the principal this week.

3. Partner Reading: Repeated Reading (Checkout Opportunity)

While students do Partner Reading, listen to individuals read the passage.

Work on accuracy and fluency, as needed.

4. Homework: Repeated Reading

Have students read the story at home.

EXTRA PRACTICE 2

Unit 14 Fluency Passage

Name _____

Fluency Passage

My goal is to read with 0–2 errors and ____ words correct per minute.

I read with ____ errors and ____ words correct per minute.

Bob and Betty

Bob and Betty flew through the dark night sky, wings billowing back and forth. They whistled, clicked, and snorted. They were searching for a new roost. — 12, 23, 26

"We must find a roost where there's lots of prey," said Bob. "Crunchy beetles are my favorite." — 39, 43

"Bob, you're always thinking about food!" said Betty. "Our new home must be warm and cozy for our new baby. It must keep us protected from predators too." — 53, 67, 71

They saw a big red house below. Bob peeked in a window. A lady wearing pink fuzzy slippers was reading a book. A cat napped in her lap. — 85, 99

Betty saw a box high on the side of the house. She flew over to it and landed. She folded her flexible wings and looked inside the box. "This looks like a perfect roost," she said. "Bob, we've located our new home!" — 116, 128, 141

Homework
I've listened to my child read this passage twice.   Date _____   Signed _____

104

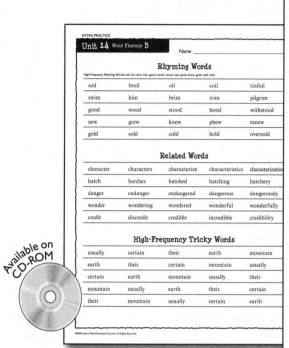

Available on CD-ROM

Unit 14 Word Fluency B

Name _____

Rhyming Words

High-Frequency Rhyming Words: soil, oil, swim, him, good, wood, stood, new, grew, knew, gold, cold, hold

soil	broil	oil	coil	tinfoil
swim	him	brim	trim	pilgrim
good	wood	stood	hood	withstood
new	grew	knew	phew	renew
gold	sold	cold	hold	oversold

Related Words

character	characters	characterize	characteristics	characterization
hatch	hatches	hatched	hatching	hatchery
danger	endanger	endangered	dangerous	dangerously
wonder	wondering	wondered	wonderful	wonderfully
credit	discredit	credible	incredible	credibility

High-Frequency Tricky Words

usually	certain	their	earth	mountain
earth	their	certain	mountain	usually
certain	earth	mountain	usually	their
mountain	usually	earth	their	certain
their	mountain	usually	certain	earth

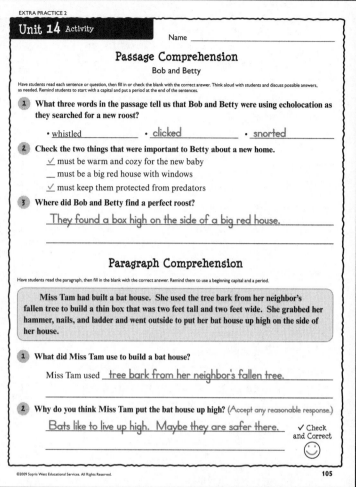

Unit 14 Activity

Name _____

Passage Comprehension
Bob and Betty

Have students read each sentence or question, then fill in or check the blank with the correct answer. Think aloud with students and discuss possible answers, as needed. Remind students to start with a capital and put a period at the end of the sentences.

1 **What three words in the passage tell us that Bob and Betty were using echolocation as they searched for a new roost?**

• whistled _____ • clicked _____ • snorted _____

2 **Check the two things that were important to Betty about a new home.**

✓ must be warm and cozy for the new baby
___ must be a big red house with windows
✓ must keep them protected from predators

3 **Where did Bob and Betty find a perfect roost?**

They found a box high on the side of a big red house. _____

Paragraph Comprehension

Have students read the paragraph, then fill in the blank with the correct answer. Remind them to use a beginning capital and a period.

> Miss Tam had built a bat house. She used the tree bark from her neighbor's fallen tree to build a thin box that was two feet tall and two feet wide. She grabbed her hammer, nails, and ladder and went outside to put her bat house up high on the side of her house.

1 **What did Miss Tam use to build a bat house?**

Miss Tam used tree bark from her neighbor's fallen tree. _____

2 **Why do you think Miss Tam put the bat house up high?** (Accept any reasonable response.)

Bats like to live up high. Maybe they are safer there. _____

✓ Check and Correct ☺

105

PROCEDURES

For each step, demonstrate and guide practice, as needed. Then have students complete the page independently.

1. Activity

Passage Comprehension

• Have students read each sentence or question, then fill in or check the blank with the correct answer.
• Think aloud with students and discuss the multiple-choice options, as needed.

Paragraph Comprehension

• Have students read the paragraph.
• Have students read each numbered sentence, then fill in the blank.
• Have students read the completed sentences.

Self-monitoring

Have students read and check their work, then draw a happy face in the Check and Correct circle.

2. Word Fluency (BLMs are located on the CD.)

• To build fluency, have students read Rhyming Words, Related Words, and High-Frequency Tricky Words. Have students read each section three times in a row.
• To build accuracy, have students read all sets with partners.

> **ACCURACY BEFORE FLUENCY (Reminder)**
>
> Word Fluency is designed to build accuracy and fluency. Students should practice for accuracy before working on fluency.

PROCEDURES

1. Sounds
Use selected Sound Cards from Units 1–14.

2. Sounding Out Smoothly
- For each word, have students say the underlined part, sound out the word smoothly, then read the whole word. Use the words in sentences, as needed.
- Have students read all the words in the row, building accuracy first, then fluency.
- Repeat practice.

3. Accuracy and Fluency Building
- For each task, have students say any underlined part, then read each word.
- Set a pace. Then have students read the whole words in each task and column.
- Repeat practice, building accuracy first, then fluency.

4. Tricky Words
Have students read each row for accuracy, then fluency.

5. Multisyllabic Words
For each word, have students read each syllable out loud, then tell how many syllables are in the word. If needed, use the word in a sentence. Have students read the whole word.

6. Dictation

best, guest, guess, truck, stuck, struck

- Say "best." Have students say the word. Have students touch or write the sounds, then read the word. Say something like:

  The first word is **best.** Say the word. (best)

  What's the first sound? (/b/) Touch under /b/.
  What's the next sound? (/ĕĕĕ/) Write /ĕĕĕ/.
  What's the next sound? (/sss/) Touch under /sss/.
  What's the last sound? (/t/) Touch under /t/.
  Read the word. (best)

- Repeat with "guest" and "guess."
- Continue with the rhyming words: truck, stuck, struck.

EXTRA PRACTICE 3

Unit 14 Decoding Practice

Name _____

1. SOUND REVIEW Use selected Sound Cards from Units 1–14.

2. SOUNDING OUT SMOOTHLY Have students say the underlined part, sound out and read each word, then read the row.

| h<u>ur</u>t | m<u>o</u>th | d<u>ar</u>k | n<u>igh</u>t |

3. ACCURACY/FLUENCY BUILDING Have students say any underlined part, then read each word. Next, have students read the column.

A1 Mixed Practice	B1 Word Endings	C1 Bossy E	D1 Related Words
l<u>ay</u>	sunny	<u>u</u>se	imagined
h<u>ea</u>d	bounces	h<u>e</u>re	imagining
c<u>o</u>ld	decided	h<u>o</u>pe	imagination
b<u>ow</u>l	lifted	c<u>a</u>ve	fascinated
apple	yawned	m<u>a</u>kes	fascinating
whist<u>le</u>	sensed		fascination
sleep<u>y</u>	glanced	n<u>i</u>ce	
drows<u>y</u>	impressed	qu<u>i</u>te	locate
alway<u>s</u>		besi<u>d</u>es	location
bette<u>r</u>		sunsh<u>i</u>ne	echolocation

4. TRICKY WORDS Have students read each row for accuracy, then fluency.

| wondered | says | nothing | listen | have | 5 |
| movement | their | your | eyes | don't | 10 |

5. MULTISYLLABIC WORDS Have students read the word by parts, tell how many syllables are in the word, then read the whole word.

Ⓐ	scrag•gly	scraggly	kitch•en	kitchen
Ⓑ	fi•nal•ly	finally	cu•ri•ous	curious
Ⓒ	scrump•tious	scrumptious	noc•tur•nal	nocturnal

6. DICTATION Say the word. Guide students as they say and segment the word. Have students say each sound as they touch or write it.

A1 Shifty Words	B1 Rhyming Words
b <u>e</u> s t	t r <u>u</u> <u>c</u> <u>k</u>
g <del>u</del> e s t	s t <u>u</u> <u>c</u> <u>k</u>
g u e <u>s</u> <u>s</u>	s t r <u>u</u> <u>c</u> <u>k</u>

©2009 Sopris West Educational Services. All Rights Reserved.

106

CAUTION

Your children may not need Extra Practice. Use assessment results to determine if Extra Practice is needed.

PROCEDURES

1. First Reading

Mix group and individual turns, independent of your voice. Have students work toward an accuracy goal of 0–2 errors and practice any difficult words.

2. Second Reading, Short Passage Practice: Developing Prosody

- Demonstrate how to read a line or two with expression. Read at a rate slightly faster than the students' rate. Say something like:

  Listen as I read the first two sentences with expression and phrasing. I'm going to emphasize certain words and pause between sentences.

  "Miss Tam was reading a book about bats as Old Scraggly Cat lay in her lap.

  'Bats are fascinating,' she said to the drowsy cat."

- Guide practice with your voice.
  Now read the paragraph with me.

- Provide individual turns while others track with their fingers and whisper read. Provide descriptive and positive feedback.
  [Anand], you read with wonderful expression!

3. Partner Reading: Repeated Reading (Checkout Opportunity)

While students do Partner Reading, listen to individuals read the passage. Work on accuracy and fluency, as needed.

4. Homework: Repeated Reading

Have students read the story at home.

EXTRA PRACTICE 3

Unit 14 Fluency Passage

Name _____

Fluency Passage

My goal is to read with 0–2 errors and ____ words correct per minute.

I read with ____ errors and ____ words correct per minute.

Miss Tam Learns About Bats

Miss Tam was reading a book about bats as Old Scraggly Cat lay in her lap. — 14, 16

"Bats are fascinating," she said to the drowsy cat. "It says here that bats are nocturnal. They use echolocation to find food in the dark. They make sounds and listen for the echo each sound makes as it bounces off their prey. Imagine that!" — 29, 42, 56, 60

Old Scraggly Cat lifted his head and yawned. Miss Tam knew he was not impressed. "Cats don't have to whistle or snort to locate food," she said to the sleepy cat. "Besides, there's always something scrumptious in your food bowl in the kitchen." — 73, 86, 97, 103

Just then, Miss Tam sensed a movement at the window. She glanced over at the dark glass. "There's nothing there. It was just my imagination, I guess," she said. "I do hope some bats find my new bat house!" — 114, 127, 141, 142

Homework
I've listened to my child read this passage twice. Date _____ Signed _____

107

PROCEDURES

For each step, demonstrate and guide practice, as needed. Then have students complete the page independently.

1. Activity

Passage Comprehension

- Have students read each sentence or question, then fill in the blank with the correct answer.
- Think aloud with students and discuss the multiple-choice options, as needed.

Paragraph Comprehension

- Have students read the paragraph.
- Have students read each numbered question, then fill in the blank.
- Have students read the completed sentences.

Self-monitoring

Have students read and check their work, then draw a happy face in the Check and Correct circle.

2. Word Fluency (BLMs are located on the CD.)

You may wish to have students repeat practice with Extra Practice, Word Fluency A or B.

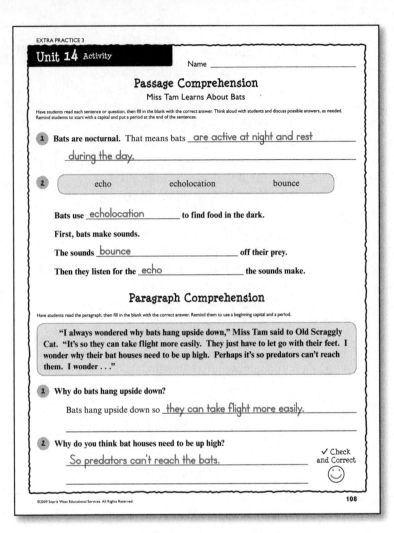

EXTRA PRACTICE 3

Unit 14 Activity

Name _____

Passage Comprehension
Miss Tam Learns About Bats

Have students read each sentence or question, then fill in the blank with the correct answer. Think aloud with students and discuss possible answers, as needed. Remind students to start with a capital and put a period at the end of the sentences.

1. Bats are nocturnal. That means bats _are active at night and rest_ _during the day._

2. | echo | echolocation | bounce |

Bats use _echolocation_ to find food in the dark.

First, bats make sounds.

The sounds _bounce_ off their prey.

Then they listen for the _echo_ the sounds make.

Paragraph Comprehension

Have students read the paragraph, then fill in the blank with the correct answer. Remind them to use a beginning capital and a period.

> "I always wondered why bats hang upside down," Miss Tam said to Old Scraggly Cat. "It's so they can take flight more easily. They just have to let go with their feet. I wonder why their bat houses need to be up high. Perhaps it's so predators can't reach them. I wonder . . ."

1. Why do bats hang upside down?

   Bats hang upside down so _they can take flight more easily._

2. Why do you think bat houses need to be up high?

   So predators can't reach the bats.

   ✓ Check and Correct ☺

108